TRASH into TREASURE

Recycling Ideas for Library/Media Centers

by ELEANOR SILVERMAN

The Scarecrow Press, Inc.
Metuchen, N.J., & London 1982

Also by Eleanor Silverman:
101 MEDIA CENTER IDEAS

Library of Congress Cataloging in Publication Data

Silverman, Eleanor, 1927-
　Trash into treasure.

　1. Instructional materials centers--United
States--Handbooks, manuals, etc.　2. Salvage
(Waste, etc.)--Handbooks, manuals, etc.　I. Title.
Z674.5.U5S52　　　　027.8'222　　　　81-18198
ISBN 0-8108-1489-7　　　　　　　　　　AACR2

Copyright © 1982 by Eleanor Silverman
Manufactured in the United States of America

To my husband, George,
who never throws anything away

TABLE OF CONTENTS

Introduction		viii
1.	Recycling Art Objects: Art for Home Use	3
2.	Recycling Books: Feltboard Stories	5
3.	Recycling Books: Paperback Exchange	7
4.	Recycling Books: Storyteller's File	8
5.	Recycling Books: Tracing Pictures	9
6.	Recycling Books and Cassette Tapes: Paperback and Cassette Set	11
7.	Recycling Bottles: Candlestick	13
8.	Recycling Bottles: Finger Puppets from Plastic Pill Bottles	15
9.	Recycling Bottles: Flower Vases	17
10.	Recycling Bottles: Terrarium	19
11.	Recycling Boxes: Book Holders	21
12.	Recycling Boxes: Dioramas	23
13.	Recycling Boxes: Finger-Puppet Stage	25
14.	Recycling Boxes: Storage	26
15.	Recycling Boxes: Theater-in-Round Props	27
16.	Recycling Brown Bags: Book Protectors	29
17.	Recycling Brown Bags: Masks	31
18.	Recycling Calendars: Tracing Calendar Pictures	33
19.	Recycling Candles: Story-Hour Candle	35
20.	Recycling Cardboard: Animal Costuming	37
21.	Recycling Cardboard: Christmas-Tree Birds	38

22.	Recycling Cardboard:	Body Puppets	39
23.	Recycling Cardboard:	Feltboard Making	41
24.	Recycling Cardboard:	Outsize Study-Print Envelopes	43
25.	Recycling Cardboard:	Puppet Making--Outline Form	45
26.	Recycling Cardboard:	Puppet-Storage Hand	47
27.	Recycling Cardboard:	Puzzle Making	49
28.	Recycling Cardboard:	Story Mobiles	51
29.	Recycling Cardboard Tubes:	Puppet Making--Construction Paper	53
30.	Recycling Cardboard Tubes:	Repair Caddy	55
31.	Recycling Cardboard Tubes:	Theater-in-Round Props	57
32.	Recycling Cassette Tapes:	Cassette Tapes for Home Use of Particular Students	58
33.	Recycling Cassette Tapes:	Interest Centers	59
34.	Recycling Cassette Tapes:	Music-Listening Station	60
35.	Recycling Cassette Tapes:	Theater-in-Round Sound Effects	61
36.	Recycling Catalogs:	Catalog-Picture Tracing	62
37.	Recycling Cloth:	Puppets	63
38.	Recycling Clothing:	Book Reports in Costume	65
39.	Recycling Clothing:	Costume Collection	67
40.	Recycling Clothing:	Storyteller's Costume	69
41.	Recycling Clothing:	Theater-in-Round Costumes	71
42.	Recycling Crockery:	Crockery Planters	72
43.	Recycling Curtains:	Puppet-Stage Curtain	73
44.	Recycling Ditto Sheets:	Announcements and Notices	75
45.	Recycling Ditto Sheets:	Card-Catalog Scrap Sheets	77
46.	Recycling Ditto Sheets:	Ditto Doodle Pad	78
47.	Recycling Ditto Sheets:	Doodle Display	79
48.	Recycling Ditto Sheets:	Make Your Own Bookmarks	81
49.	Recycling Ditto Sheets:	Puppet-Play Writing--Rough Copy	82
50.	Recycling Ditto Sheets:	Theater-in-Round Play Writing--Rough Copy	83

51.	Recycling Dolls: Storytelling with a Doll	85
52.	Recycling Egg Cartons: Finger-Puppet Storage	87
53.	Recycling Egg Cartons: Organizer Tray	89
54.	Recycling Egg Cartons: Walking Storybook Characters	90
55.	Recycling Foam-Plastic Packaging: Foam Book Holder	91
56.	Recycling Foam-Plastic Packaging: Foam Organizer Tray	93
57.	Recycling Games: Backgammon	94
58.	Recycling Games: Checkers	95
59.	Recycling Games: Chess	97
60.	Recycling Games: Scrabble	98
61.	Recycling Looseleaf Binders: Record of Bibliographies	99
62.	Recycling Looseleaf Binders: Record of Instruction Dittos	100
63.	Recycling Looseleaf Binders: Storage for Theater-in-Round Scripts	101
64.	Recycling Magazines: Magazine Articles for Verticle File	103
65.	Recycling Magazines: Magazine Giveaway	104
66.	Recycling Maps: Maps for Student Borrowing	105
67.	Recycling Newspapers: Book-Jacket Mobile	107
68.	Recycling Newspapers: Make Your Own Cartoon	109
69.	Recycling Newspapers: Newspaper Clippings	110
70.	Recycling Newspapers: Tabletop Protection	111
71.	Recycling Newspapers: That Was the Week That Was	113
72.	Recycling Pillows: Reading Corner	115
73.	Recycling Plastic Cups: Christmas-Tree Bells	117
74.	Recycling Plastic Hose Eggs: Easter Eggs	118
75.	Recycling Plastic Lids: Christmas-Tree Ornaments	119
76.	Recycling Puzzles: Puzzles for Home Use	120
77.	Recycling Records: Background Music	121
78.	Recycling Report-Card Envelopes: AV Containers	123
79.	Recycling Scrapbook Covers: Special Album	125
80.	Recycling Shoe Bags: Puppet Holder	127
81.	Recycling Stuffed Animals: Storytelling with Stuffed Animals	129

82.	Recycling Suitcases: Costume Collection	130
83.	Recycling Suitcases: Environmental Kit	131
84.	Recycling Suitcases: Puppet Storage	132
85.	Recycling Wire Hangers: Display	133
86.	Recycling Wood Boards: Puzzle Board	135
Index		136

INTRODUCTION

Although recycling has been much talked about for the last few years, it did not become a special interest of mine until a year ago. I was asked to represent the Little Silver, N.J., School District at a local recycling meeting at Red Bank Regional High School. As I drove back to Point Road School after the meeting, it occurred to me how much could be recycled in a media center, and how important a role the media specialist could assume in influencing patrons to recycle materials.

The term "recycling," as used in this book, means using a material again in its original form or making it into a new product. Every day media centers throughout our country throw away boxes, cartons, cardboard, and bottles that can, with little time and effort, be reused or converted into new products. All it takes is a little imagination and the desire to be part of an environmental cleanup. Become aware of what is being thrown out or discarded in your media center. Ask yourself, "Can any of these materials be reused? Can a new product be created from any of these discarded items?"

In addition, media specialists, because of their positions on school staffs, can influence teachers, students, administrators, parents, and visitors by fostering the awareness of the need to clean up the environment. You can set an example not only by recycling materials through programs and activities but also by making environmental books, pamphlets, and other materials available for personal borrowing as well as classroom use.

Trash into Treasure is a ready-reference collection of recycling ideas that proved successful at the Point Road School media center. Inexpensive but creative, each project is presented in an easy-to-follow recipe form, with step-by-step directions, materials required, length of time needed for completion, and suggestions to ensure success. The Table of Contents lists the ideas alphabetically by material being recycled. A detailed index makes it easy to locate specific ideas. All of the projects are adaptable to any elementary media center. Readers can follow the "recipes" as presented, combine them, or join them with ideas of their own.

Recycling materials will enhance media-center programs and activities. Cardboard can become animal costuming (20), body puppets (22), puppet-storage hands (26), puzzles (27), and feltboards (23). Cartons, with little time and effort, become props for Theater-in-Round productions: tables, time machines, caves, apple barrels, or spaceships. Cardboard tubes become puppets (29) or oars and canes (31). Cassette tapes, easily erased, can be reused in a variety of activities, from interest centers (33) to student instruction (32). Paperbacks can stimulate reading through an exchange (3) or in combination with cassettes (6). Old clothing can become costumes not only for students (39) but for an imaginative media specialist (40). Outgrown Halloween costumes can become part of a costume collection available for use in plays or special programs (39).

Throwaway items can be transformed into attractive media-center decorations: crockery into flowerpots (42), lamp globes into vases (9), plastic cups (73) and lids (75) into Christmas ornaments, and plastic egg containers for hose into Easter eggs (74).

Parents are happy to donate many items that their children have outgrown: games, records, checkerboards, paperback books. Alert your Parent Teacher Organization to the items you are looking for. Select those that you wish to use and give away the rest. Many students and teachers appreciate media-center giveaways.

In addition to its obvious benefits on the environment, recycling also has a positive effect upon media-center budgets. With budgets dwindling as costs of books, AV materials, and supplies rise, it becomes important to be economical and recycle whatever you can. Savings can then go to purchase those materials needed to keep the quality of your program intact.

My deep appreciation to Kathy MacLean, a parent assistant, who took the photographs for this book. All photos were taken in the Point Road School media center.

Many thanks to my husband, George, to whom this book is dedicated, and to my superintendent, Mr. Edward A. Pavlovsky, for his continued interest and encouragement.

ELEANOR SILVERMAN
August 1981

TRASH
INTO
TREASURE

Recycling Ideas for Library/Media Centers

Illus. 1: Bookcase containing art objects and puzzles to be circulated

1. RECYCLING ART OBJECTS: ART FOR HOME USE

Participants: Media specialist; parent assistants; students

Location: Media center

Time span: 20-30 minutes

Purposes:
1) To expose students to art
2) To make it possible for students to borrow art objects

Materials:
Date-due slip
Framed picture (ready to hang)
Legend of picture (artist, title of work, synopsis of artist's life)

Procedure:
1) Ask parent assistant to investigate picture and prepare legend.
2) Ask student to assist by pasting legend and date-due slip on back of picture.
3) Place where it will be noticed.
4) Students may borrow art objects in the same manner as a book or record.

Suggestions:
1) Ask Parent Teacher Organization to solicit donations of unwanted art objects to the media-center collection. Select and use only appropriate objects.
2) Display art attractively.

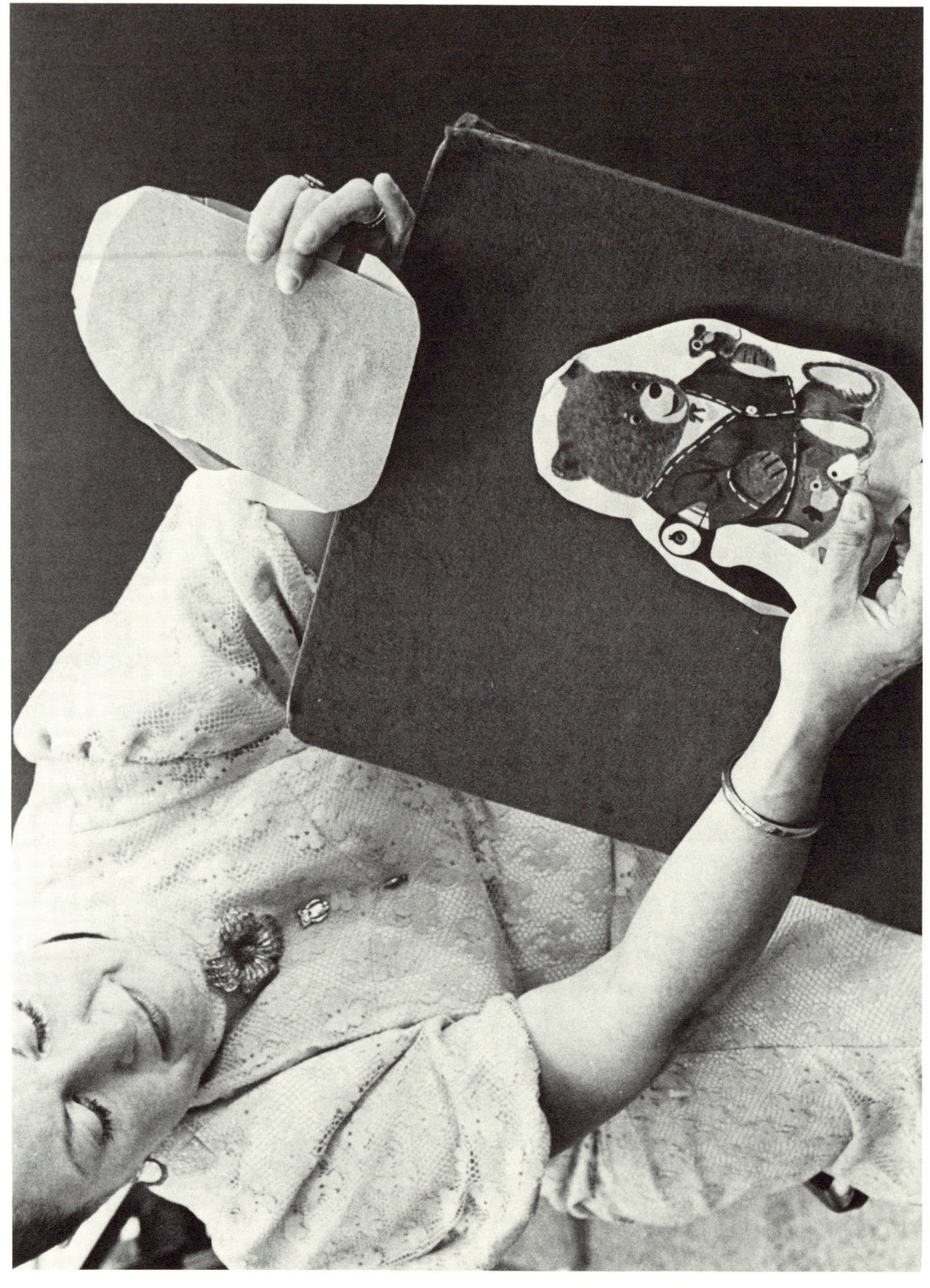

Illus. 2: Feltboard story made from an old book

2. RECYCLING BOOKS: FELTBOARD STORIES

Participants: Media specialist; parent assistants; students

Location: Media center

Time span: 30 minutes

Purposes: 1) To encourage students to do storytelling
                2) To improve hand-and-eye coordination
                3) To stimulate imagination of students

Materials: Glue
                Newspapers
                Old books
                Old pictures
                Sandpaper
                Scissors

Procedure: 1) Cover table with newspapers.
                2) Ask parent assistants to provide "extra hands" for students who need assistance.
                3) Direct students in cutting out pictures.
                4) Direct students in cutting sandpaper into strips.
                5) Direct students in pasting sandpaper strips on back of pictures (rough side of sandpaper must be facing out).
                6) Allow pictures to dry overnight before use.

Suggestions: 1) Teach students to use feltboard pictures with a feltboard.
                2) Teach students to pace pictures with storytelling.
                3) Effective in grades 2, 3, 4 as a group or class project.

Illus. 3: Students using the Paperback Exchange

3. RECYCLING BOOKS: PAPERBACK EXCHANGE

Participants:	Media specialist; students
Location:	Media center
Time span:	15 minutes
Purposes:	1) To encourage students to read 2) To give students access to many paperbacks
Materials:	Box (attractive) Paperback books (donated)
Procedures:	1) Ask Parent Teacher Organization to remind parents to donate paperbacks no longer read by their children. 2) Select appropriate paperbacks to be used. 3) Choose attractive box. 4) Print PAPERBACK EXCHANGE on sides of box. 5) Place donated paperbacks in box. 6) Put box where students will notice it. 7) Tell classes: any student may exchange a paperback for a paperback in box.
Suggestions:	1) Students may donate paperbacks also.

4. RECYCLING BOOKS: STORYTELLER'S FILE

Participants: Media specialist

Location: Media center

Time span: 30 minutes

Purposes:
1) To provide file of stories for media specialist to learn or to read to classes
2) To stimulate imagination of students
3) To interest students in stories

Materials:
Envelope (manila, large)
Old books
Scissors
Stapler

Procedure:
1) Remove stories from books.
2) Staple pages of each story together.
3) Place each story in manila envelope marked STORY-TELLER'S FILE

Suggestions:
1) Tell or read stories by candlelight.
2) For candle and candlestick see illus. 7.

5. RECYCLING BOOKS: TRACING PICTURES

Participants: Media specialist; students

Location: Media center

Time span: 10 minutes

Purposes:
1) To prevent marring of library furniture and materials
2) To give students enjoyment
3) To relax students who are under pressure

Materials:
Crayons
Easel
Pictures
Tracing paper

Procedure:
1) Remove pictures from discarded books.
2) Place pictures, tracing paper, and crayons on easel (or in carrel).
3) Students may keep tracings when they have been colored and completed.

Suggestions:
1) Catalogs and calendars may be used (see illus. 18).
2) Brown onionskin sheets found in dittos make good tracing paper.

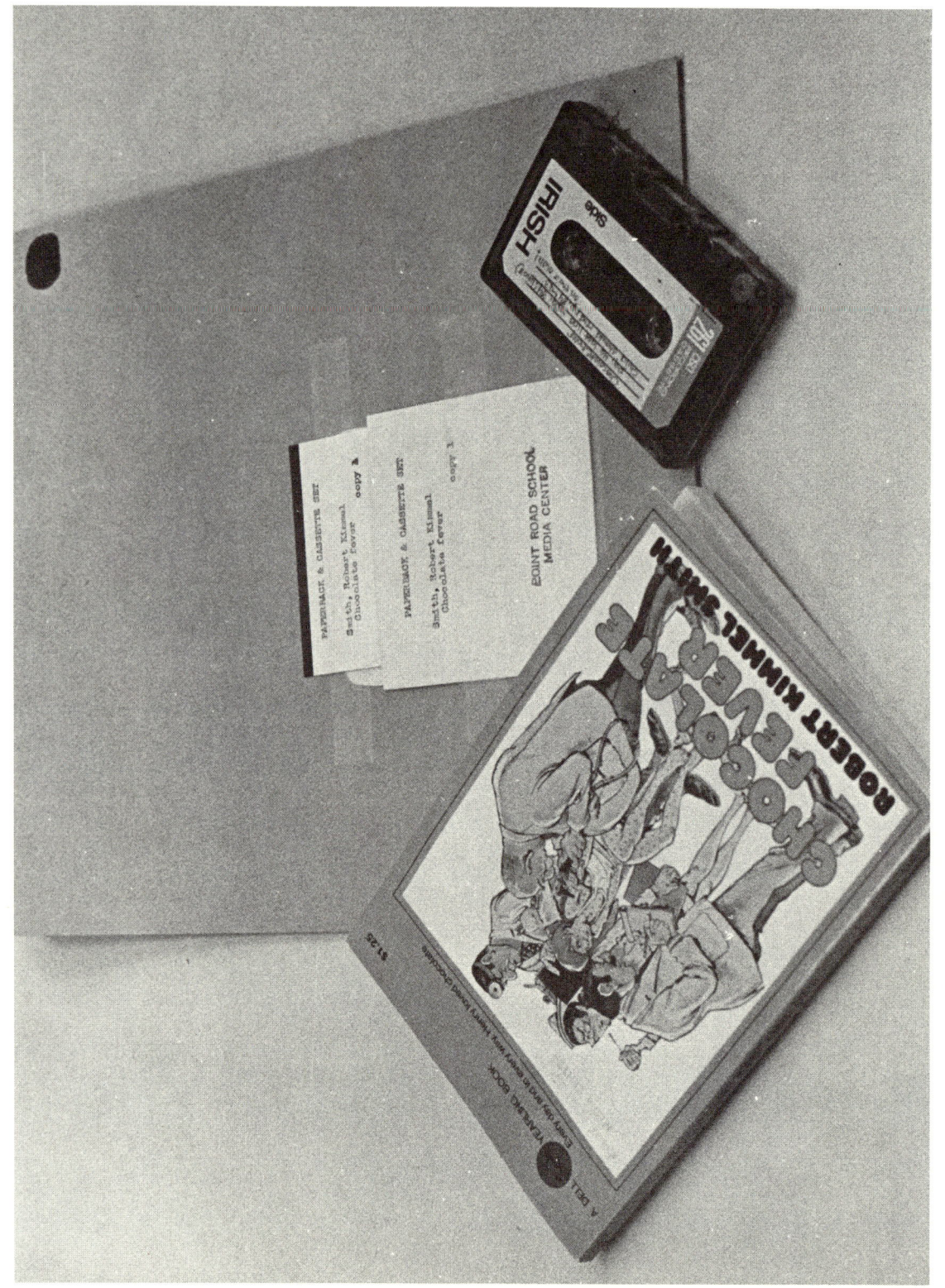

Illus. 6: Paperback and cassette set ready for student use

6. RECYCLING BOOKS AND CASSETTE TAPES:
   PAPERBACK AND CASSETTE SET

Participants:	Media specialist
Location:	Media center
Time span:	30-45 minutes
Purposes:	1) To stimulate students who have difficulty reading
Materials:	Book (paperback, donated) Book card and pocket Cassette recorder Cassette tape (erased) Envelope (manila) Scotch tape
Procedure:	1) Record book on cassette tape. 2) Package book and tape together in manila envelope. 3) Attach book card and pocket to envelope with scotch tape. 4) Allow students to borrow set.
Suggestions:	1) Especially effective with Title I and Classified students.

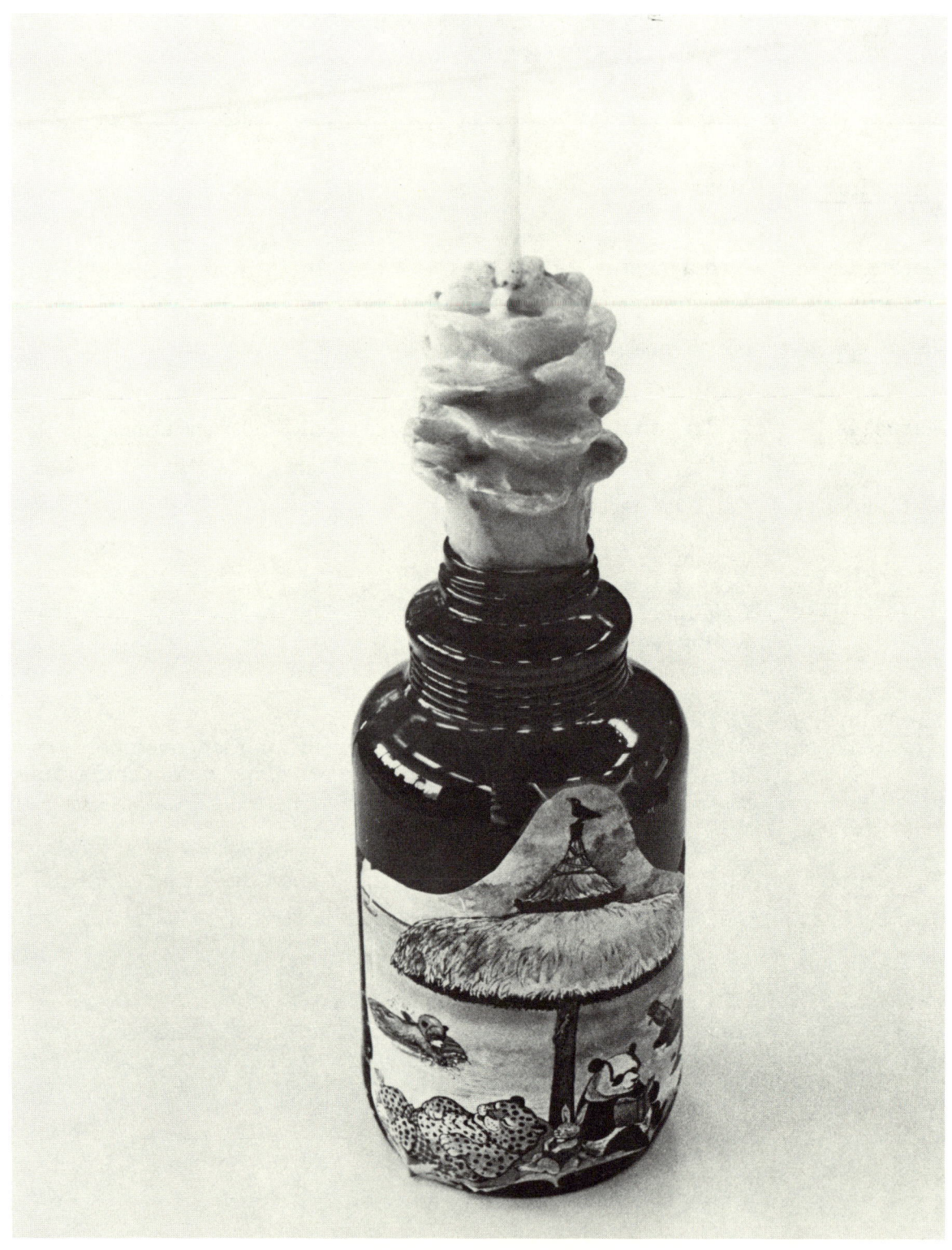

Illus. 7: Candlestick and candle for storytelling

7. RECYCLING BOTTLES: CANDLESTICK

Participants: Media specialist; parent assistants

Location: Media center

Time span: 10 minutes

Purposes: 1) To enhance storytelling with candlelight
                2) To add warm and homey atmosphere to story hour

Materials: Bottle (attractive shape)
                Picture
                Tape (clear)

Procedure: 1) Wash bottle thoroughly.
                2) Soak bottle to remove label.
                3) Dry bottle.
                4) Tape picture on bottle.

Suggestions: 1) Create an unusual candle for your candlestick (see idea 19).

8. RECYCLING BOTTLES: FINGER PUPPETS FROM PLASTIC PILL BOTTLES

Participants:	Media specialist; students
Location:	Media center or classroom
Time span:	20 minutes
Purposes:	1) To improve hand-and-eye coordination 2) To stimulate creativity of students 3) To provide outlet for self-expression of students
Materials:	Paste Pictures (from magazines, book brochures, old books) Plastic pill bottles (without caps) Strips of colored paper
Procedure:	1) Each student receives plastic pill bottle, and strip of colored paper. 2) Each student pastes strip on body of bottle, leaving top and bottom of bottle uncovered. 3) Each student selects picture and pastes it on colored strip. 4) Each student uses magic markers to enhance picture.
Suggestions:	1) Prepare materials in advance of session. 2) May be used successfully in grades 2, 3, 4 as a small-group or whole-class activity. 3) Good activity for a storytelling workshop for students.

Illus. 9: Globe of a broken lamp makes an attractive vase with artificial flowers

9. RECYCLING BOTTLES: FLOWER VASES

Participants: Media specialist; parent assistants

Location: Media center

Time span: 10 minutes

Purposes: 1) To add attractiveness to media-center furnishings
                 2) To add warmth to media center

Materials: Bottle (attractive shape)
                 Flowers (fresh or artificial)

Procedure: 1) Wash bottle thoroughly.
                 2) Soak bottle to remove label.
                 3) Dry bottle; add flowers.
                 4) Place on bookcase or other furniture.

Suggestions: 1) Leftover globes of table lamps are effective with artificial flowers.

10. RECYCLING BOTTLES: TERRARIUM

Participants: Media specialist; parent assistants

Location: Media center

Time span: 15 minutes

Purposes:
1) To add attractiveness to media center
2) To add warmth to media-center furnishings

Materials:
Bottle (large)
Pebbles
Plant (small)
Potting soil

Procedure:
1) Clean bottle thoroughly; remove label.
2) Place pebbles ($\frac{1}{2}$-inch) on bottom inside bottle.
3) Cover pebbles with two inches of potting soil.
4) Place plant on soil; cover roots with soil.
5) Add another inch of potting soil around plant.
6) Water carefully; do not drown plant.

Suggestions:
1) Choose a bottle with a large-enough opening for hand to fit in.

Illus. 11: Tissue-box book holder in use

11. RECYCLING BOXES: BOOK HOLDERS

Participants: Media specialist; classroom teacher; students

Location: Media center; classroom

Time span: 10 minutes

Purposes:
1) To encourage students to build their own book collections
2) To encourage students to set aside time each day to read

Materials:
Pencil
Ruler
Scissors
Tissue box

Procedure:
1) Mark with pencil and ruler how much opening must be enlarged to hold books.
2) Cut as marked, enlarging opening.
3) Stand books up in enlarged opening.

Suggestions:
1) Choose colorful tissue boxes.
2) Good as an individual, small-group, or whole-class activity.
3) Effective in grades 2, 3, 4, 5.

Illus. 12: Box recycled as a diorama

12. RECYCLING BOXES: DIORAMAS

Participants: Media specialist; classroom teacher; students

Location: Media center; classroom

Time span: 30 minutes

Purposes:
1) To create interesting book reports
2) To create meaningful media-center displays
3) To interest students in reading books depicted in dioramas

Materials:
Boxes (shoe)
Crayons
Magic markers
Paper (construction)
Paste
Pencils
Scissors

Procedure:
1) Each student receives shoe box and piece of construction paper.
2) Each student draws scene he/she wishes to display on construction paper; colors scene; cuts it to fit inside of box.
3) Each student pastes scene to inside of box.
4) Students add small planes, cars, figurines, and others as desired.
5) Exhibit dioramas when ready.

Suggestions:
1) Each student attaches the following information to diorama: author and title of book and scene depicted.

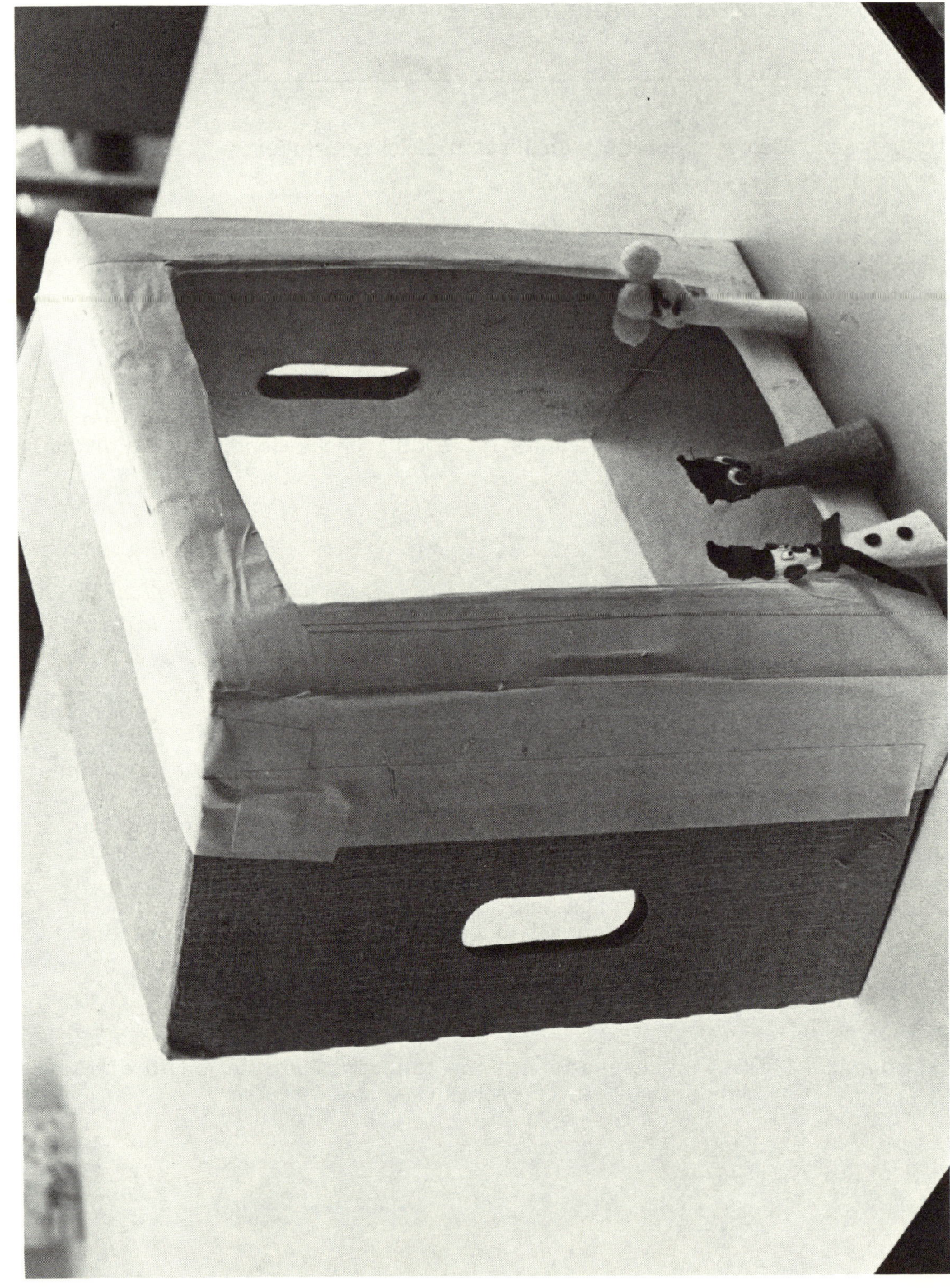

Illus. 13: Box recycled as a finger-puppet stage

13. RECYCLING BOXES: FINGER-PUPPET STAGE

Participants: Media specialist; students

Location: Media center; classroom

Time span: 20 minutes

Purposes: 1) To enhance use of finger puppets
2) To stimulate creativity of students

Materials: Box
Magic markers
Scissors
Tape (colored)

Procedure: 1) Select box of appropriate size.
2) Turn box over so bottom is visible.
3) Mark outline of opening to be cut out of bottom.
4) Cut around outline; remove piece cut out.
5) Cut off any flaps of box.
6) Students decorate puppet stage with magic markers and colored tape.

Suggestions: 1) Puppet stage can easily be carried to classrooms.

14. RECYCLING BOXES: STORAGE

Participants:	Media specialist
Location:	Media center
Time span:	As needed
Purposes:	1) To keep center neat 2) To hold AV neatly on shelves
Materials:	Boxes (appropriate size) Magic marker
Procedure:	1) Decide what is to be stored. 2) Determine appropriate size and number of boxes. 3) Gather boxes and label with magic marker. 4) Place materials in boxes. 5) Place boxes in appropriate areas.
Suggestions:	1) Boxes make appropriate storage for AV materials when integrating shelving. Any kind of box can be used provided it fits on your shelves: shoe boxes, small cartons, tote boxes, etc.

15. RECYCLING BOXES: THEATER-IN-ROUND PROPS

Participants: Media specialist; students

Location: Media center

Time span: 10 minutes

Purposes: 1) To add realism to play

Materials: Box (cardboard)
Magic markers (if needed)

Procedure:
1) Students in play decide on props and substitutes that can be used in place of props difficult to obtain such as apple barrels, time machines, caves, etc.
2) Students decorate and rehearse with substitute props.

Suggestions: 1) Students may take substitute props after play performance.

Illus. 16: Brown grocery bags protect materials from damage

16. RECYCLING BROWN BAGS: BOOK PROTECTORS

Participants: Media specialist; parent assistants

Location: Media center

Time span: 5 minutes

Purposes:
1) To educate students to protect media-center materials
2) To protect media-center materials from rain and snow

Materials:
Bags (brown grocery)
Magic marker
Shopping bag (with handles)
Wire hanger

Procedure:
1) Print on shopping bag with magic marker: PROTECT YOUR BOOKS FROM RAIN AND SNOW. PLEASE USE A BAG.
2) Fill shopping bag with brown grocery bags.
3) Hang shopping bag by handles on a wire hanger.
4) Hang near bookcase or checkout desk.

Suggestions:
1) Large grocery bags can also protect records, study prints, and multimedia sets.

17. RECYCLING BROWN BAGS: MASKS

Participants: Media specialist; students

Location: Media center; classrooms

Time span: 15-20 minutes

Purposes:
1) To dispense with costumes
2) To add to interest of play for audience

Materials:
Bags (large brown grocery)
Crayons
Magic markers
Scissors

Procedure:
1) Each student receives shopping bag.
2) Each student draws face on one side of bag.
3) Each student colors face, hair, etc.
4) Eyes are cut out.
5) Each student slips bag over head to try it.

Suggestions:
1) Can be used effectively in theater-in-round plays.
2) Can be used as a small-group or whole-class activity.
3) Effective in grades 2, 3, 4.

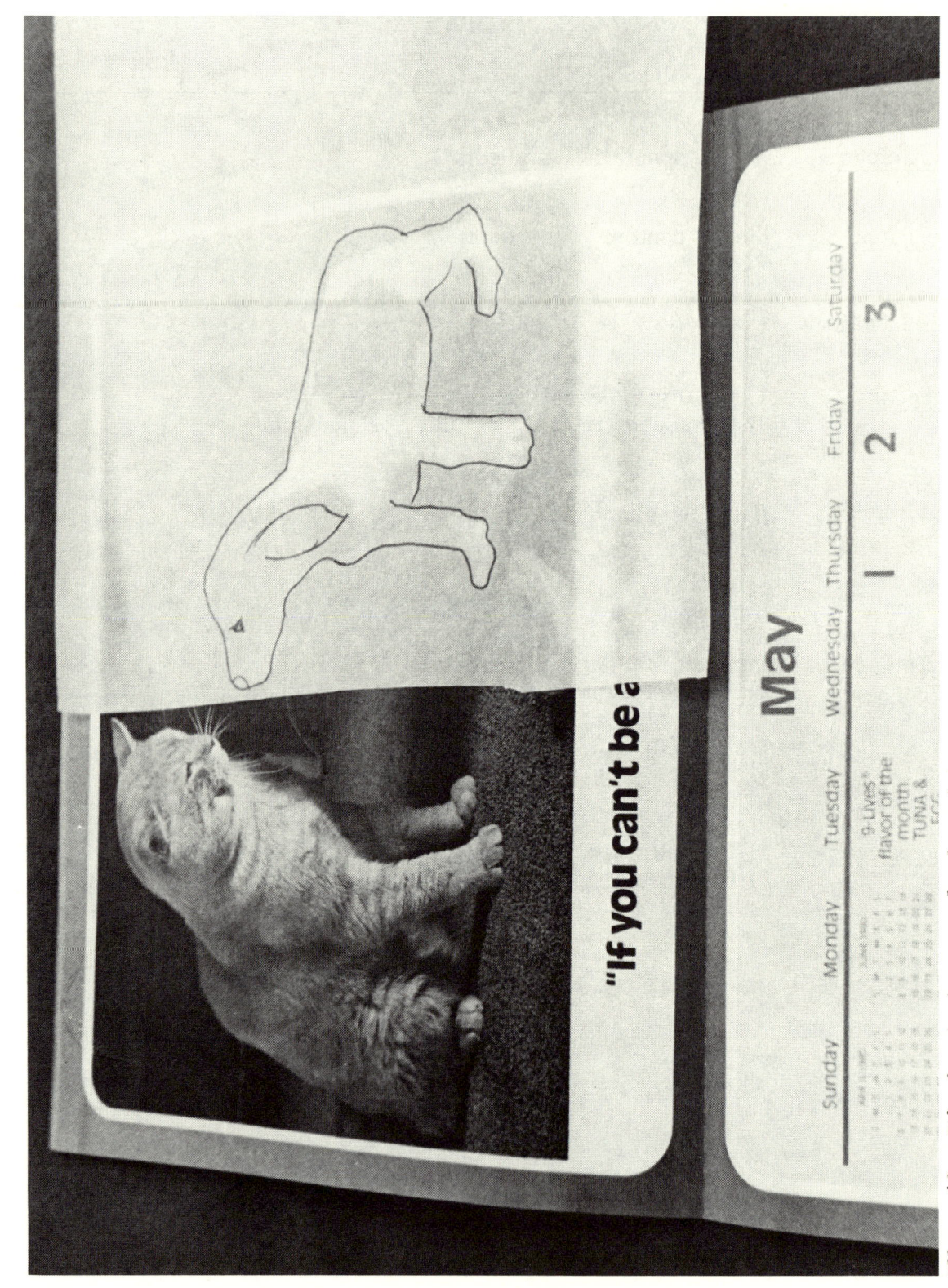

Illus. 18: It's fun to trace calendar pictures

18. RECYCLING CALENDARS: TRACING CALENDAR PICTURES

Participants: Media specialist; parent assistants; students

Location: Media center

Time span: 10 minutes

Purposes:
1) To prevent marring of furniture and materials
2) To give students enjoyment
3) To relax students under pressure

Materials:
Calendars (past)
Onionskin sheets
Pencils (colored)

Procedure:
1) Place newspaper on desk of carrel.
2) Place a past calendar, several sheets of onionskin, and some colored pencils on the newspaper.
3) Add a sign to the carrel: HAVE FUN TRACING.
4) Students may keep tracings when completed.

Suggestions:
1) Choose calendars with appealing pictures.
2) Brown onionskin from dittos makes good tracing paper.

19. RECYCLING CANDLES: STORY-HOUR CANDLE

Participants: Media specialist

Location: Media center

Time span: 5 minutes

Purposes:
1) To create warm atmosphere for story hour
2) To make story hour a special time for students

Materials: Candles (used, different widths)
Matches

Procedure:
1) Apply lighted match to bottom of narrowest candle until wax softens.
2) Place wax softened-side-down onto wider candle.
3) Apply lighted match to bottom of wider candle until wax softens.
4) Place wax softened-side-down onto opening of bottle or onto other candlestick.

Suggestions:
1) For story-hour candle and candlestick see illus. 7.

Illus. 20: Cardboard ears and tail for a donkey

20. RECYCLING CARDBOARD: ANIMAL COSTUMING

Participants: Media specialist; students

Location: Media center

Time span: 10-15 minutes

Purposes:
1) To dispense with full costumes
2) To add to interest of play for audience

Materials:
Cardboard
Magic markers
Safety pins
Scissors
Stapler

Procedure:
1) Discuss animal in play with participating students: characteristics of ears, tail, etc.
2) Draw outline of ears, tail, etc., of animal on cardboard.
3) Cut around outlines freeing ears, tail, etc., from cardboard.
4) Students color ears, tail, etc., with magic markers.
5) Measure head size of student who will portray animal in the play.
6) Cut a band of cardboard to fit around student's head.
7) Staple ears to band; staple ends of band so band is complete circle.
8) Attach tail to student with safety pins.

Suggestions:
1) Effective in theater-in-round productions with grades 2, 3, 4.

21. RECYCLING CARDBOARD: CHRISTMAS-TREE BIRDS

Participants: Media specialist; students

Location: Media center

Time span: 20 minutes

Purposes: 1) To provide Christmas-tree ornaments made by students
                  2) To provide enjoyable activity for students

Materials: Cardboard
                  Cord
                  Paste
                  Picture (bird)
                  Scissors

Procedures: 1) Students paste bird pictures on cardboard.
                  2) Allow several minutes to dry.
                  3) Cut around pictures, following shape of pictures and making certain to cut through cardboard.
                  4) Students poke hole through each picture, making certain hole is through cardboard backing.
                  5) Students slip piece of cord through each hole; tie small loop.
                  6) Students hang each bird ornament on Christmas tree.

Suggestions: 1) Effective as a small-group activity.

22. RECYCLING CARDBOARD: BODY PUPPETS

Participants: Media specialist; students

Location: Media center

Time span: 20 minutes

Purposes:
1) To stimulate imagination of students
2) To stimulate creativity of students

Materials:
Cardboards (large)
Crayons
Magic markers
Pencils
Scissors

Procedure:
1) Outline with pencil holes to be cut on each cardboard for student's face and hands.
2) Help students cut out holes for face and hands.
3) Students decorate cardboards with crayons and magic markers.
4) Students don their body puppets.
5) Students take turns at role playing.

Suggestions:
1) Especially effective with Title I groups; also younger students.

23. RECYCLING CARDBOARD: FELTBOARD MAKING

Participants: Media specialist; students

Location: Media center

Time span: 15 minutes

Purposes: 1) To interest students in storytelling
2) To provide board for feltboard stories

Materials: Cardboards (from shirts or packing boxes)
Felt
Glue
Scissors

Procedure: 1) Cover table with newspaper.
2) Place cardboard on newspaper.
3) Put glue on cardboard, especially edges and corners.
4) Smooth felt over glue.
5) Turn cardboard over.
6) Repeat above procedure.
7) Allow feltboard to dry overnight before use.

Suggestions: 1) Coordinate with feltboard stories (see idea 2).

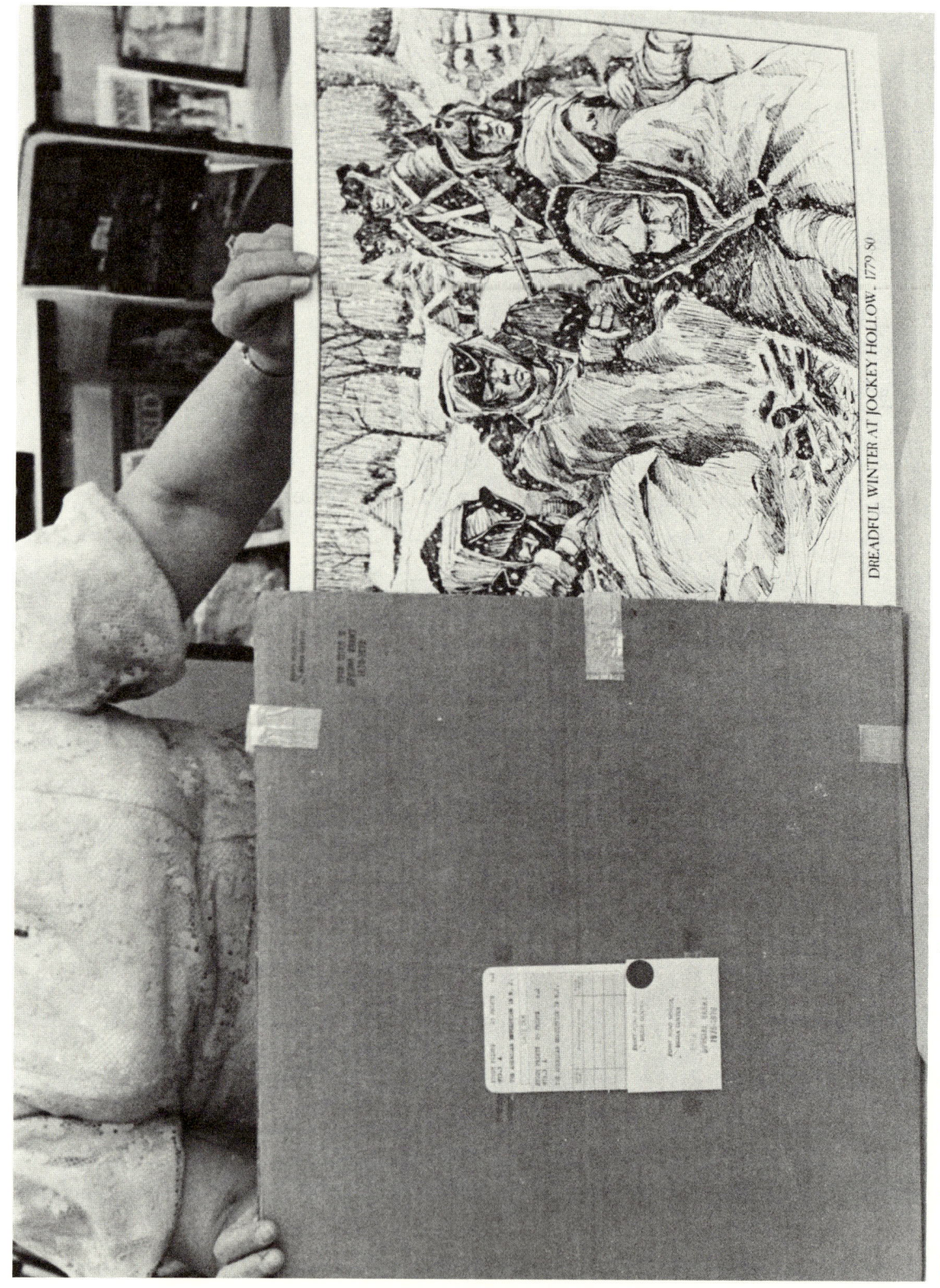

Illus. 24: Cardboard envelope for outsize prints

24. RECYCLING CARDBOARD: OUTSIZE STUDY-PRINT ENVELOPES

Participants: Media specialist

Location: Media center

Time span: 10 minutes

Purposes:
1) To provide packaging for outsize prints
2) To permit circulation of outsize prints

Materials:
Cardboard (large)
Magic marker
Tape
Scissors

Procedure:
1) Choose two pieces of cardboard larger than prints.
2) Cut pieces of cardboard so they are the same size.
3) Tape bottoms and two sides of cardboards together, leaving tops untaped.
4) Slip prints into cardboard envelope through untaped top.

Suggestions:
1) Add book pocket and card to cardboard envelope to circulate study prints.

25. RECYCLING CARDBOARD: PUPPET MAKING--OUTLINE FORM

Participants: Media specialist

Location: Media center

Time span: 10 minutes

Purposes: 1) To facilitate making puppets

Materials: Cardboard
Pencil
Scissors

Procedure: 1) Draw form of puppet you wish students to make.
2) Cut out form neatly.

Suggestions: 1) Students may trace outline form on construction paper or material.

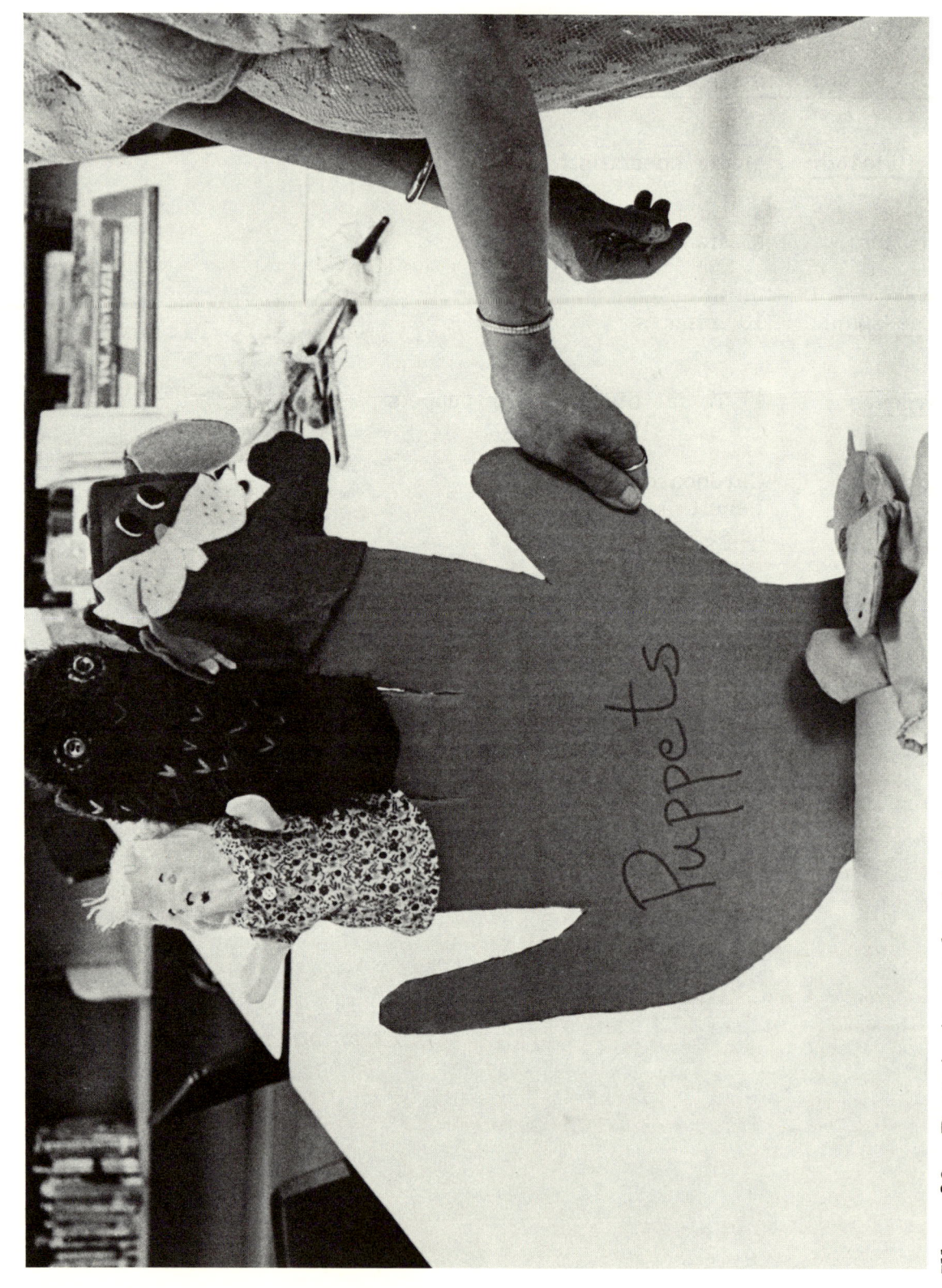

Illus. 26: Puppet-storage hand in use

26. RECYCLING CARDBOARD: PUPPET-STORAGE HAND

Participants: Media specialist

Location: Media center

Time span: 10 minutes

Purposes:
1) To store hand puppets attractively
2) To keep hand-puppet collection visible and available to students

Materials:
Cardboard (large)
Pencil
Scissors

Procedure:
1) Draw an outline of a hand on the cardboard; spread fingers of hand.
2) Cut around outline, freeing hand from cardboard.
3) Set hand up in appropriate spot.
4) Place a hand puppet on each finger.

Suggestions:
1) Old shoe bags make good puppet storage also (see illus. 80).

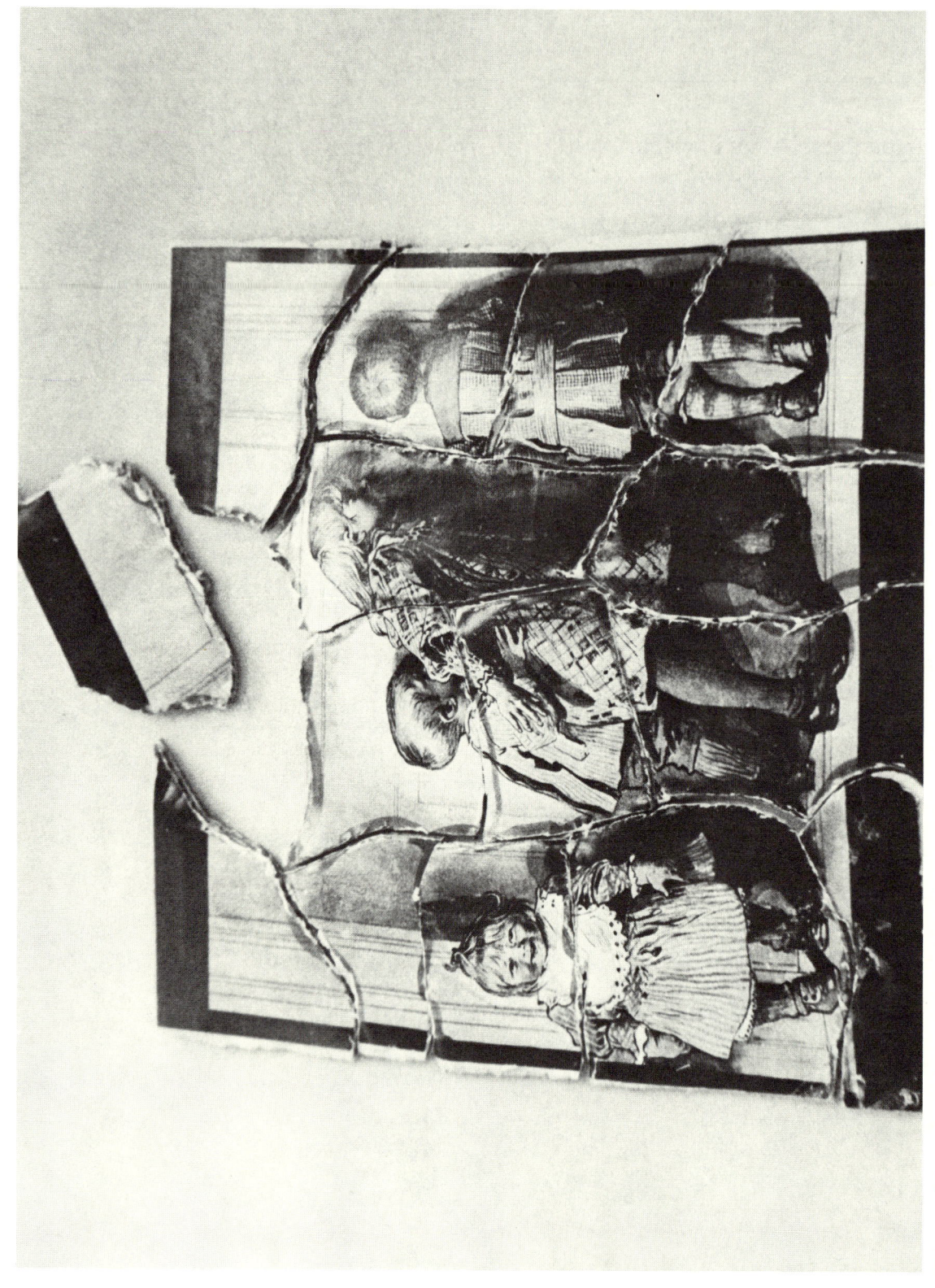

Illus. 27: Puzzle made with piece of cardboard

27. RECYCLING CARDBOARD: PUZZLE MAKING

Participants: Media specialist; students

Location: Media center

Time span: 15-20 minutes

Purposes: 1) To provide fun activity for students

Materials: Cardboards (from shirts or packing materials)
Glue
Magic markers
Pictures (magazines)
Scissors

Procedure:
1) Each student receives cardboard and picture.
2) Students glue pictures on cardboards.
3) Students use magic markers to outline shapes of puzzle pieces each picture will be cut into.
4) Students cut along magic-marker outlines.
5) Students may keep their puzzles.

Suggestions:
1) Easily coordinated with social-studies units: geography, history, holidays.

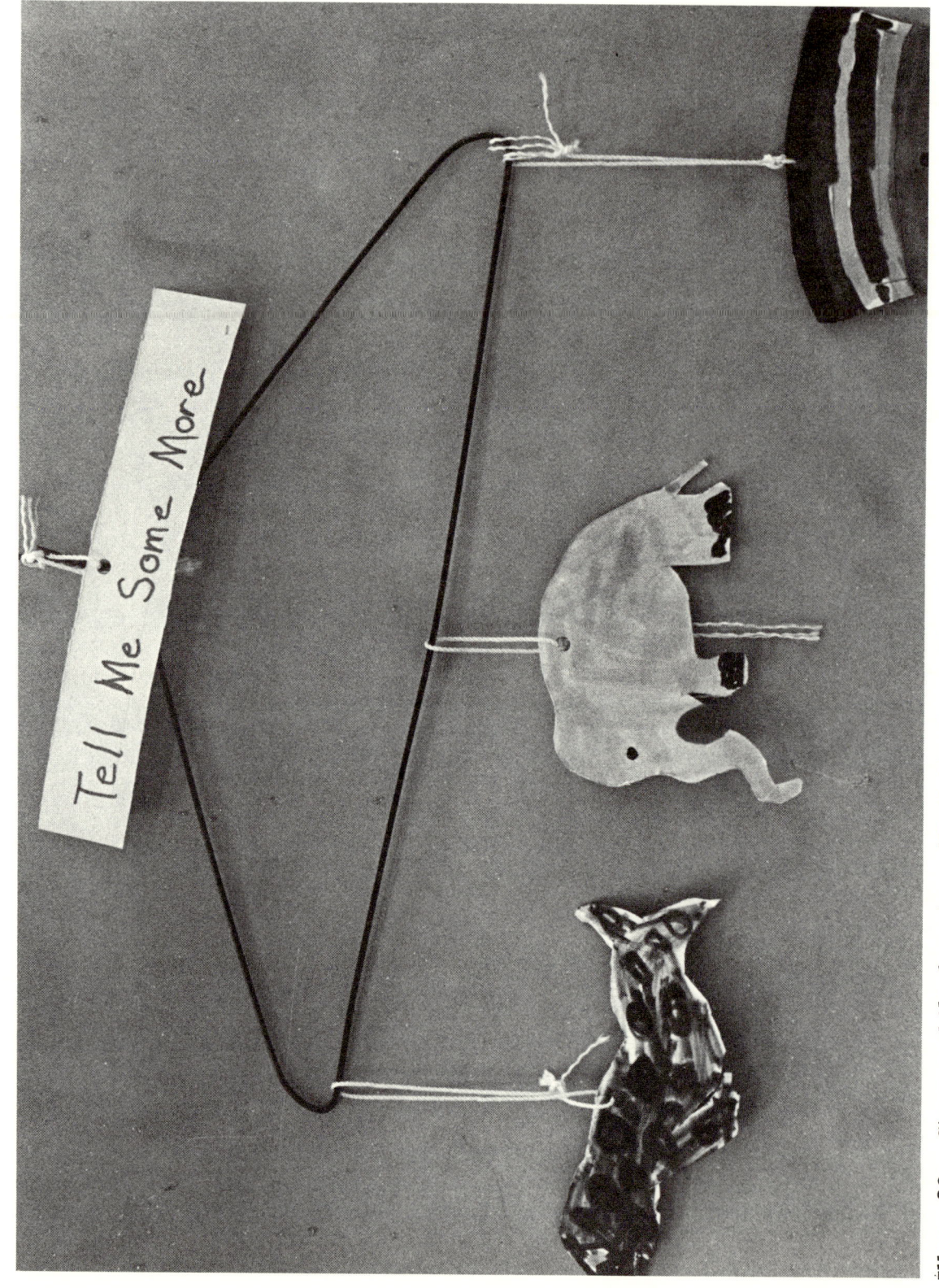

Illus. 28: Story mobile for story "Tell Me Some More"

50

28. RECYCLING CARDBOARD: STORY MOBILES

Participants: Media specialist; students

Location: Media center; classroom

Time span: 30 minutes

Purposes:
1) To provide another form for book reports
2) To provide attractive and meaningful decorations

Materials:
Cardboard
Cord
Magic markers
Pencils
Scissors
Wire hangers

Procedure:
1) Each student receives cardboard and pencil.
2) Students draw pictures on cardboard associated with stories read.
3) Students color pictures with magic markers.
4) Students cut out pictures.
5) Students poke holes in pictures and thread cord through each hole.
6) Pictures are tied to wire hangers.
7) Each student prints name of book on cardboard and ties it to hanger above pictures.
8) Hang wire hangers for display.

Suggestions:
1) Effective in grades 2, 3.

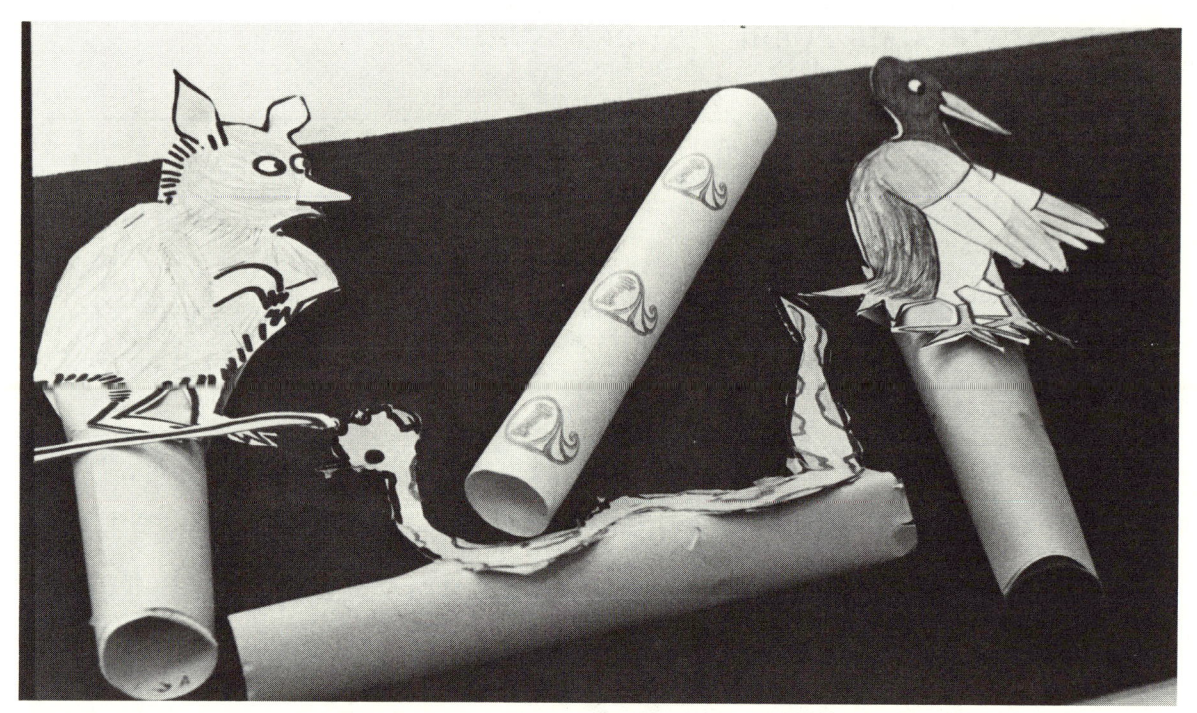

Illus. 29A: Construction-paper puppets with cardboard tubes

Illus. 29B: Students display construction-paper dinosaur puppets coordinated with dinosaur reports

52

29. RECYCLING CARDBOARD TUBES: PUPPET MAKING--
    CONSTRUCTION PAPER

Participants: Media specialist; classroom teachers; parent assistants; students

Location: Media center; classroom

Time span: 30 minutes

Purposes:
1) To improve hand-and-eye coordination
2) To stimulate creativity of students
3) To provide outlet for self-expression of students

Materials:
Construction paper
Cut-out forms
Magic markers
Paste
Stapler
Tubes (from toilet-paper or paper-towel rolls)

Procedure:
1) Each student receives sheet of construction paper; each folds sheet in half.
2) Each student receives cut-out form to trace on sheet of construction paper.
3) Students use magic markers to draw faces, clothing, etc.
4) Students use crayons to color figures.
5) Students cut out puppet figures, cutting through both halves of construction paper.
6) Put paste on tube and insert it between both halves of figure.
7) Staple both halves together. (One half becomes front of puppet; one half is back.)
8) Students apply finishing touches.
9) Allow one day to dry thoroughly.

Suggestions:
1) Puppets may be coordinated with characters in books, plays, short stories, as well as history or geography lessons in classroom.
2) Many hands are needed, so arrange to have extra help.

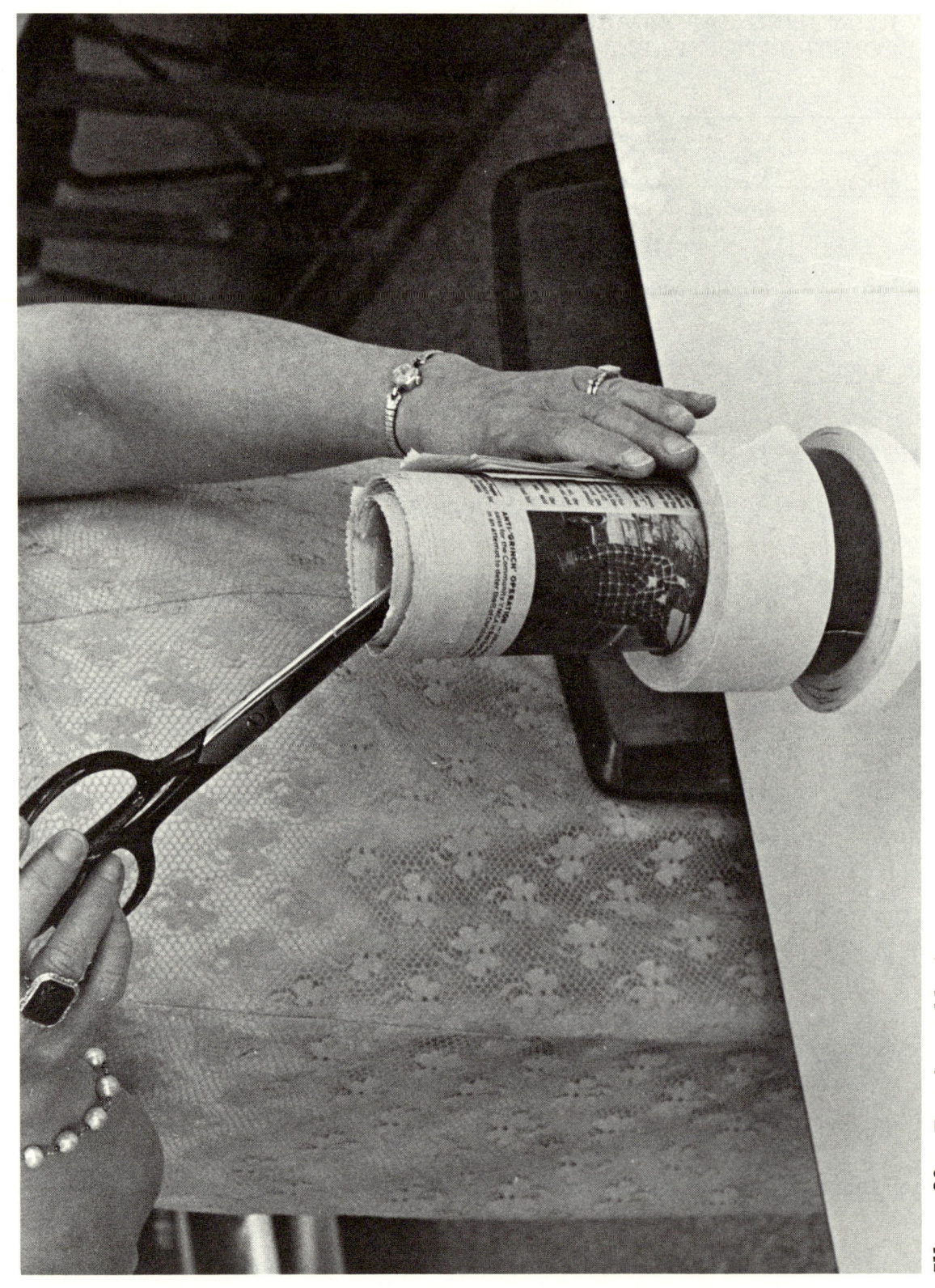

Illus. 30: Repair caddy in use

30. RECYCLING CARDBOARD TUBES: REPAIR CADDY

Participants:	Media specialist
Location:	Media center
Time span:	10 minutes
Purposes:	1) To have repair materials close at hand 2) To have repair materials in one place 3) To have repair materials take as little space as possible
Materials:	Newspapers Scissors Tapes Tube (from paper towels)
Procedure:	1) Wrap newspapers tightly around tube, leaving top and bottom openings uncovered. 2) Tape newspapers so they cannot unravel from tube. 3) Stand tube upright and place rolls of tape on tube. 4) Place scissors, blades down, in top opening of tube.
Suggestions:	1) Wrap enough newspaper around tube so rolls of tape are not too loose.

Illus. 31A: Cardboard tubes become oars for Long John Silver

Illus. 31B: Cardboard tube becomes a cane for blind pirate

31. RECYCLING CARDBOARD TUBES: THEATER-IN-ROUND PROPS

Participants: Media specialist; students

Location: Media center

Time span: 10 minutes

Purposes: 1) To add realism to play

Materials: Cardboard tubes (long)
                Magic markers (if needed)

Procedure: 1) Students in play decide on props and substitutes that can be used in place of props difficult to obtain, such as oars, guns, canes, knives, etc.
                2) Students decorate and rehearse with substitute props.

32. RECYCLING CASSETTE TAPES: CASSETTE TAPES FOR HOME USE OF PARTICULAR STUDENTS

Participants: Media specialist; classroom teacher; students

Location: Media center

Time span: 15-20 minutes

Purposes:
1) To extend instruction of particular students beyond school hours and school facilities
2) To help students achieve academic goals in shortest possible time
3) To involve families in aiding students

Materials:
Cassette tape (erased)
Cassette player
Envelope (manila)

Procedure:
1) Record lesson on cassette tape (usually by teacher).
2) Name of student to receive cassette tape given to media specialist.
3) Place cassette tape in envelope (manila).
4) Attach pocket and card to facilitate circulation.
5) Stamp out cassette tape to student.

Suggestions:
1) Erase cassette tape and record other lessons as often as needed.

33. RECYCLING CASSETTE TAPES: INTEREST CENTERS

Participants: Media specialist; parent assistants

Location: Media center

Time span: 10-15 minutes; once a month

Purposes:
1) To stimulate natural curiosity of children concerning recycling
2) To stimulate students to learn about recycling
3) To encourage students to recycle materials

Materials:
Cassette player
Cassette tape (recycled and rerecorded)
Leaflets (recycling)
Pictures (recycling)

Procedure:
1) Erase a cassette tape and record a message for students about the importance of recycling materials and what they can do.
2) Place cassette tape, cassette player, and materials concerning recycling in a carrel.
3) Attach sign to carrel: LEARN ABOUT RECYCLING AND ITS IMPORTANCE TO OUR ENVIRONMENT.

34. RECYCLING CASSETTE TAPES: MUSIC-LISTENING STATION

Participants: Media specialist

Location: Media center

Time span: 15-20 minutes; once a month

Purposes:
1) To acquaint students with aesthetic value of music
2) To help students develop appreciation for music
3) To create awareness of connection of music to all areas of life, including recycling

Materials: Cassette player
Cassette tape

Procedure:
1) Erase cassette tape and record music.
2) Place cassette player and cassette tape in a carrel.
3) Attach sign: MUSIC-LISTENING STATION; add name of composer to sign.

Suggestions:
1) May be used to individualize the school's music program, grade 3 and above.

35. RECYCLING CASSETTE TAPES: THEATER-IN-ROUND SOUND EFFECTS

Participants: Media specialist; students

Location: Media center

Time span: 15 minutes

Purposes: 1) To add interest to play for audience
2) To add realism to play

Materials: Cassette recorder
Cassette tape

Procedure: 1) Erase cassette tape.
2) Students record sound effects for play.
3) Store tape until needed.

Suggestions: 1) Erase tape after play and reuse tape with other groups.

36. RECYCLING CATALOGS: CATALOG-PICTURE TRACING

Participants: Media specialist; parent assistants; students

Location: Media center

Time span: 10 minutes

Purposes:
1) To improve hand-and-eye coordination
2) To provide fun activity for students
3) To prevent marring of furnishings

Materials:
Catalogs (Sears Roebuck, Montgomery Ward, etc.)
Magic markers
Onionskin sheets
Pencils

Procedure:
1) Place old catalogs, magic markers, onionskin sheets, and pencils on table or in carrel.
2) Attach a sign: TRACE A PICTURE AND COLOR IT.
3) Students may keep their pictures when finished.

Suggestions:
1) Brown onionskin found in dittos makes good tracing paper.
2) Calendars may also be used (see illus. 18).

37. RECYCLING CLOTH: PUPPETS

Participants: Media specialist; students

Location: Media center

Time span: 30 minutes

Purposes:
1) To improve hand-and-eye coordination
2) To stimulate creativity of students
3) To stimulate role playing of students

Materials:
Cloth (scraps)
Magic markers
Needles
Scissors
Thread (or yarn)

Procedure:
1) Make pattern of puppet shape.
2) Place pattern on double-thickness of material.
3) Cut out form.
4) Distribute puppet body, needle, and thread to each student.
5) Each student sews thicknesses of material together, leaving opening at bottom.
6) Students create face and other details with magic markers.

Suggestions:
1) For finger puppets use same procedure, but make puppets smaller.
2) Buttons can become eyes, noses, mouths, and ears.
3) Many hands are needed, especially with small children.
4) Puppets may be made for a particular story or coordinated with classroom units.
5) See finger puppets in illus. 13 and hand puppets in illus. 26.

38. RECYCLING CLOTHING: BOOK REPORTS IN COSTUME

Participants: Media specialist; classroom teacher; students

Location: Media center

Time span: 45-60 minutes

Purposes: 1) To provide interesting and different form of book report

Materials: Biographies (for student reading)
Costumes

Procedure:
1) Each student reads biography.
2) Each student chooses dates, events, and episodes to relate to others.
3) Each student dresses as character in biography.
4) Appropriate classes are invited to serve as audience.
5) Each student, in turn, dressed in costume, relates events, important dates, and some episodes of biography he or she has read.

Suggestions: 1) This program can be successfully coordinated with social studies, especially American history.

Illus. 39: Paper-tiger costume borrowed from media-center collection

39. RECYCLING CLOTHING: COSTUME COLLECTION

Participants:	Media specialist
Location:	Media center
Time span:	10-15 minutes
Purposes:	1) To have costumes available for media-center plays 2) To have costumes available for classroom plays 3) To have costumes available for students to borrow for Halloween
Materials:	Costumes Magic marker Trunk (or suitcase)
Procedure:	1) Ask Parent Teacher Organization to alert members to your need for costumes. 2) Gather costumes; fold them carefully. 3) Place costumes in old trunk or suitcase. 4) Label trunk or suitcase: COSTUME COLLECTION.
Suggestions:	1) Collect all types of costumes, including those made out of paper costumes. 2) A carton box may be used in place of a trunk or suitcase.

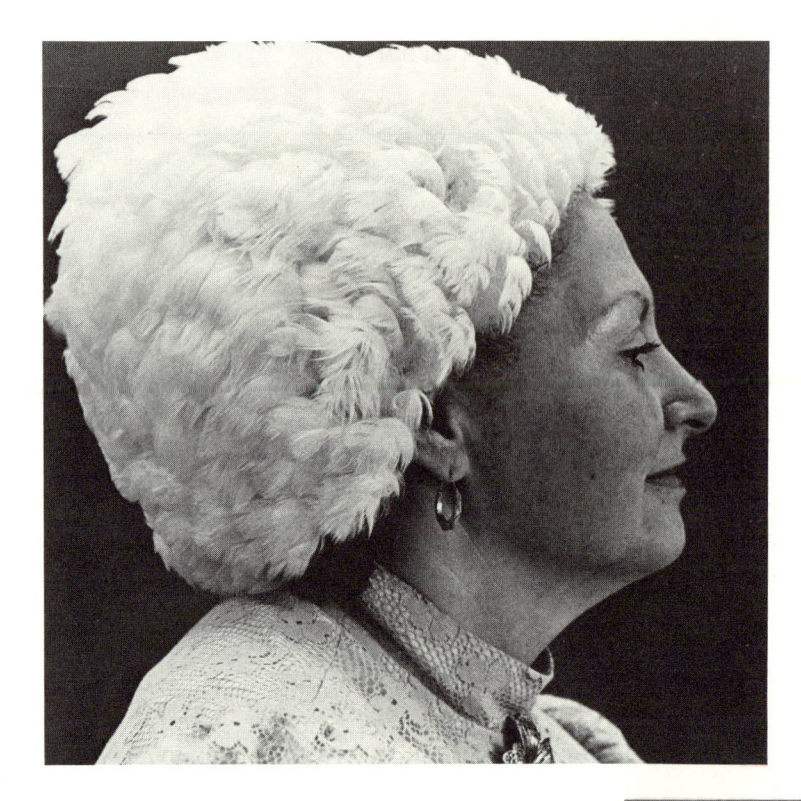

Illus. 40A: Media specialist, in donated feather-net hat, prepares for special program

Illus. 40B:
Gay Nineties outfit
of media specialist
created from
recycled clothing

40. RECYCLING CLOTHING: STORYTELLER'S COSTUME

Participants: Media specialist; student storytellers

Location: Media center

Time span: 10-15 minutes

Purpose:
1) To add atmosphere to story hour
2) To make story hour special

Materials: As required by costume

Procedure:
1) Decide on costume to use.
2) Gather items of costume (from costume collection or elsewhere).
3) Decide on date and time of story hour in which to wear costume.
4) Wear costume for particular story hour.

Suggestions:
1) Costumes may be worn for holiday story hours, special poetry sessions, etc. (see illus. 40A).
2) Costumes may be adopted as the daily dress of the media specialist. Media specialist of Point Road School dresses daily in Gay Nineties attire (see illus. 40B).

Illus. 41A:
Media specialist
ties a kerchief
on the head of
a pirate

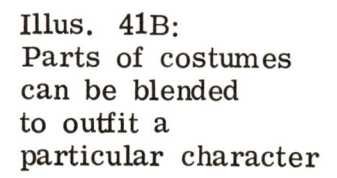

Illus. 41B:
Parts of costumes
can be blended
to outfit a
particular character

70

41. RECYCLING CLOTHING: THEATER-IN-ROUND COSTUMES

Participants: Media specialist; students

Location: Media center

Time span: 10-15 minutes

Purposes: 1) To add realism to play

Materials: As needed in play

Procedure:
1) Discuss character in play to decide distinctive items of clothing to be used.
2) Browse through media-center costume collection.
3) Remove items to be used.
4) Replace items after use.

Suggestions: 1) For animal costuming see illus. 20.

42. RECYCLING CROCKERY: CROCKERY PLANTERS

Participants: Media specialist; parent assistants

Location: Media center

Time span: 10 minutes

Purposes:
1) To add attractiveness to media center
2) To remind students and teachers to recycle whatever materials they can

Materials:
Crockery
Pebbles
Plant
Potting soil

Procedure:
1) Clean crockery thoroughly.
2) Place pebbles on bottom of inside of crockery.
3) Add several inches of potting soil.
4) Place plant on potting soil; cover roots with potting soil.
5) Fill crockery with potting soil, leaving one inch unfilled.
6) Water plant carefully; do not drown plant.

Suggestions:
1) Teapots and large pottery cups and vases make interesting planters.

43. RECYCLING CURTAINS: PUPPET-STAGE CURTAIN

Participants: Media specialist

Location: Media center

Time span: 15-30 minutes

Purposes: 1) To provide attractive and inexpensive puppet-stage curtain

Materials: Curtain
Measuring tape
Needle
Thread

Procedures: 1) Choose curtain to be converted into puppet-stage curtain.
2) Measure area of puppet stage to be covered by curtain.
3) Adjust length and width of curtain by sewing seams and hem.
4) Hang curtain in puppet stage.

Suggestions: 1) Curtains add to attractiveness of puppet stage.

44. RECYCLING DITTO SHEETS: ANNOUNCEMENTS AND NOTICES

Participants: Media specialist

Location: Media center

Time span: 5 minutes

Purposes: 1) To alert students to media-center activities

Materials: Ditto sheet (reverse side)
Magic marker
Masking tape

Procedure: 1) Print announcement on reverse side of ditto sheet.
2) Attach to media-center door with masking tape.

Suggestions: 1) Use masking tape, not scotch tape. Masking tape is easy to remove and does not mar paint or varnish.

Illus. 45: Old ditto sheets recycled as card-catalog scrap sheets

45. RECYCLING DITTO SHEETS: CARD-CATALOG SCRAP SHEETS

Participants: Media specialist; parent assistants

Location: Media center

Time span: 10-15 minutes

Purposes:
1) To provide small sheets of paper for students to write call numbers on
2) To provide small pieces of paper for students to use as bookmarks

Materials:
Box (small)
Ditto sheets (used)
Magic markers
Scissors

Procedure:
1) Choose box of appropriate size.
2) Draw and color designs on box.
3) Cut dittos into size to fit into box.
4) Place scrap sheets into box.
5) Place box on card catalog for student use.

Suggestions:
1) Place pencil near scrap-sheet box to facilitate use of the scrap sheets.

46. RECYCLING DITTO SHEETS: DITTO DOODLE PAD

Participants: Media specialist; students

Location: Media center

Time span: 10 minutes

Purposes:
1) To prevent marring of furniture and materials
2) To give students acceptable area in which to doodle
3) To give students enjoyment
4) To relax students under pressure

Materials:
Crayons
Ditto sheets (used)
Easel

Procedure:
1) Staple ditto sheets together to form pad.
2) Place pad on easel.
3) Place crayons (box) on easel.
4) Write on pad: DOODLE BOOK.

Suggestions: 1) Students love doodle pads, so prepare several in advance.

47. RECYCLING DITTO SHEETS: DOODLE DISPLAY

Participants: Media specialist; students

Location: Media center

Time span: 15 minutes

Purposes: 1) To display the interesting doodles students draw in media center

Materials: Doodles (on ditto sheets)
Stapler

Procedure: 1) Collect doodles and choose those to be displayed.
2) Staple doodles to bulletin board.

Suggestions: 1) Ask students to sign doodles so all will know who drew them.
2) Student cartoons make an interesting bulletin board (see idea 68).

Illus. 48: Student creating his own bookmark

48. RECYCLING DITTO SHEETS: MAKE YOUR OWN BOOKMARKS

Participants: Media specialist; students

Location: Media center

Time span: 15 minutes

Purposes: 1) To provide bookmarks students will want to use
                2) To prevent book pages from being folded and torn

Materials: Ditto sheets (used)
                Magic markers
                Newspapers
                Scotch tape
                Tissue box (empty)

Procedure: 1) Print with magic marker on ditto sheet: MAKE YOUR OWN BOOKMARK.
                2) Attach sign to empty tissue box so it stands.
                3) Cover part of table with newspaper.
                4) Place sign on table.
                5) Cut dittos into strips; place strips on newspaper.
                6) Set out magic markers near strips.
                7) Students may keep and use bookmarks they make.

Suggestions: 1) Very effective in protecting books.

49. RECYCLING DITTO SHEETS: PUPPET-PLAY WRITING--ROUGH COPY

Participants: Media specialist; students

Location: Media center

Time span: 20 minutes

Purposes: 1) To create play for puppets

Materials: Ditto sheets (reverse side)
Pencils
Puppets (used in play)

Procedure: 1) Permit students to handle puppets they wish to use in play.
2) Discuss personality traits of characters.
3) Record students' words as well as ideas for stage directions.
4) Permit students to try out dialogue and stage directions.
5) When ready, record play on fresh ditto.

Suggestions: 1) Handling puppets will stimulate students' imaginations, and they will produce a better script.

50. RECYCLING DITTO SHEETS: THEATER-IN-ROUND PLAY WRITING--ROUGH COPY

Participants: Media specialist; students

Location: Media center

Time span: 20 minutes

Purposes: 1) To make a play production possible by writing script to be performed

Materials: Ditto sheets (reverse side)
Pencils

Procedures:
1) Gather students who will be in play.
2) Sit around table and discuss ideas for play.
3) Write outline of play.
4) Assign part to each student to be written.
5) As each part of play is completed, read it to whole group for comments, additions, suggestions.
6) Type complete play on a fresh ditto.

Suggestions: 1) Reverse sides of ditto sheets can also be used for rough copies of reports.

51. RECYCLING DOLLS: STORYTELLING WITH A DOLL

Participants:	Media specialist; students
Location:	Media center
Time span:	15 minutes
Purposes:	1) To stimulate interest in stories 2) To stimulate imagination of students
Materials:	Doll (recycled) Rubber band
Procedure:	1) Seat students on rug. 2) Introduce story. 3) Attach doll to hand with rubber band. 4) Sit on low storytelling stool. 5) Have doll help tell story.
Suggestions:	1) Dolls, in good condition, can be donated by parents. 2) Practice is required to carry on dialogue between storyteller and doll. 3) Effective in K-3. 4) For technique see illus. 81.

Illus. 52: Egg carton as puppet storage

52. RECYCLING EGG CARTONS: FINGER-PUPPET STORAGE

Participants: Media specialist; students

Location: Media center

Time span: 10 minutes

Purposes:
1) To store finger puppets in one container
2) To have finger puppets occupy least amount of space
3) To make finger puppets easily accessible to students

Materials:
Egg carton
Finger puppets
Scissors

Procedure:
1) Cut off flat lid from egg carton.
2) Place finger puppet in each compartment in bottom part of egg carton.
3) Place near finger-puppet stage so students can easily use puppets.

Suggestions:
1) Colored-plastic egg cartons make attractive finger-puppet storage.

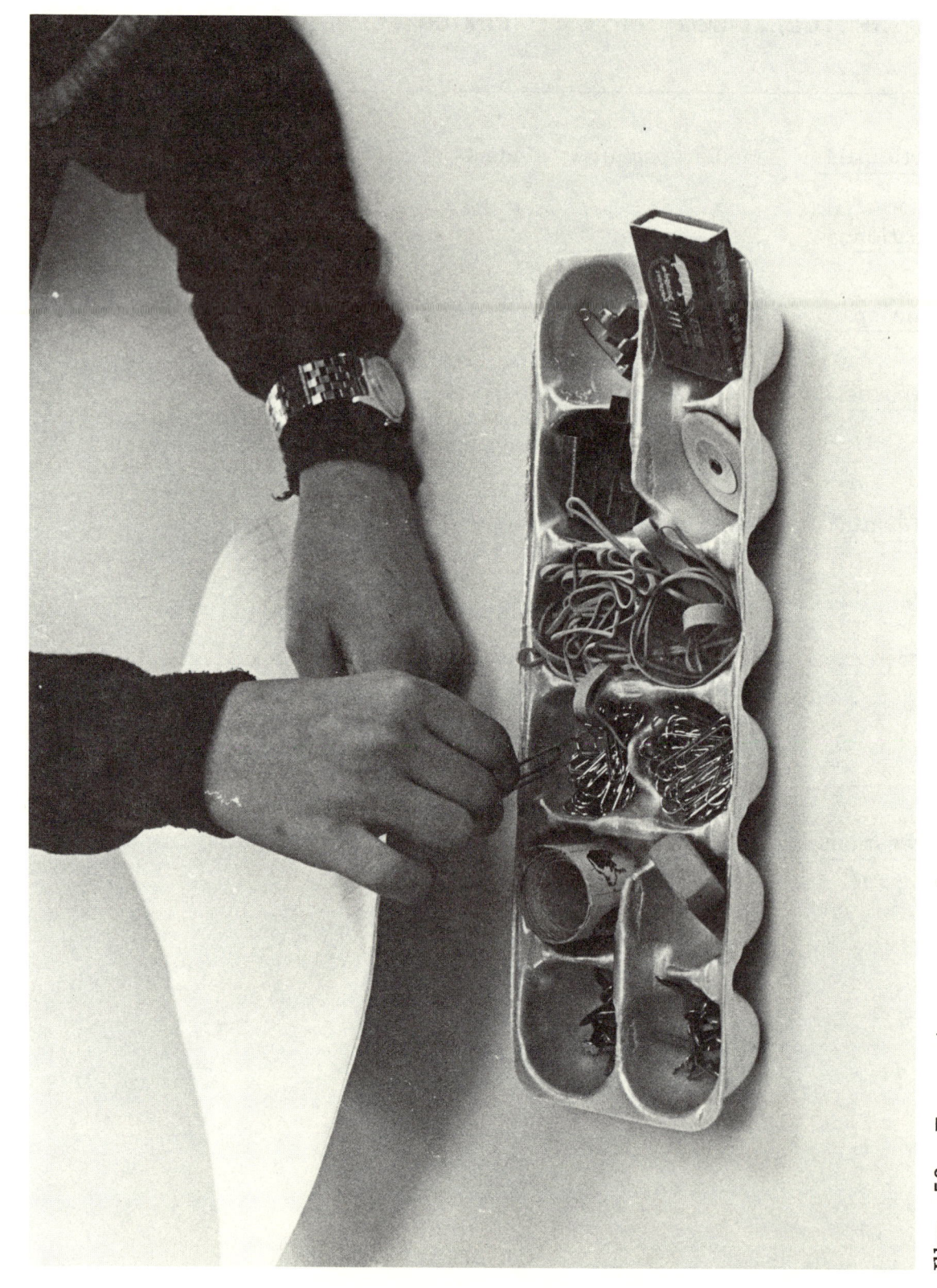

Illus. 53: Egg carton as organizer tray

53. RECYCLING EGG CARTONS: ORGANIZER TRAY

Participants: Media specialist

Location: Media center

Time span: 10 minutes

Purposes:
1) To organize small-size supplies neatly
2) To have small-size supplies available quickly

Materials:
Egg carton
Scissors

Procedure:
1) Cut off flat lid of egg carton.
2) Fill each compartment in bottom part of egg carton with necessary small-size supplies, such as clips, rubber bands, staples, safety pins.
3) Place in desk drawer.

Suggestions:
1) Colored-plastic egg cartons make attractive organizer trays.

54. RECYCLING EGG CARTONS: WALKING STORYBOOK CHARACTERS

Participants: Media specialist; students

Location: Media center

Time span: 10 minutes

Purposes: 1) To be used as another form of book reports
                 2) To provide fun activity for students

Materials: Egg cartons
                 Paste
                 Pictures (book advertisements, magazines, etc.)
                 Scissors

Procedure: 1) Only the flat lids of the egg cartons are distributed to students.
                 2) Students divide lids in half horizontally.
                 3) Students paste selected pictures on lid halves.
                 4) Students cut long thin openings near bottoms of pictures to permit fingers to be slipped through and used as feet.

Suggestions: 1) Good as a small-group activity in grades 2, 3.

55. RECYCLING FOAM-PLASTIC PACKAGING: FOAM BOOK HOLDER

Participants: Media specialist

Location: Media center

Time span: 5 minutes

Purposes: To exhibit particular book

Materials: Book
Foam packaging

Procedure: 1) Place book in depression of foam packaging in standing position.
2) Place on top of bookcase or carrel.

Suggestions: 1) Good as part of a holiday exhibit.

Illus. 56: Foam-plastic packaging in use as organizer tray

56. RECYCLING FOAM-PLASTIC PACKAGING: FOAM ORGANIZER TRAY

Participants: Media specialist

Location: Media center

Time span: 10 minutes

Purposes:
1) To organize supplies in desk drawer
2) To have supplies available quickly

Materials:
Foam packaging
Supplies (to be organized)

Procedure:
1) Fill depressions with necessary items, such as clips, rubber bands, etc.
2) Place in desk drawer.

Suggestions:
1) Easy and convenient to use.

57. RECYCLING GAMES: BACKGAMMON

Participants: Media specialist; students

Location: Media center

Timo span: 30 minutes

Purposes:
1) To provide a beneficial after-school activity
2) To stimulate interest in the media center
3) To stimulate thinking ability

Materials: Backgammon game (recycled)

Procedure:
1) Ask Parent Teacher Organization to solicit donations of used but complete backgammon sets to media center.
2) Collect as many sets as possible.
3) Students take turns with games.

Suggestions:
1) Good as after-school activity. Need at least 30 minutes to play.
2) Plan instruction session.

58. RECYCLING GAMES: CHECKERS

Participants: Media specialist; students

Location: Media center

Time span: During school day

Purposes:
1) To provide a beneficial library activity
2) To stimulate interest in the media center
3) To stimulate thinking ability

Materials: Checkerboard (recycled)
Checkers (set)

Procedure:
1) Ask Parent Teacher Organization to solicit donations of used but complete checker games to the media center.
2) Place game in the center of a library table.
3) Permit students to play any time during school day.

Suggestions:
1) This game is very popular with students, so several games are needed.
2) Checkers may also be used as an after-school activity.

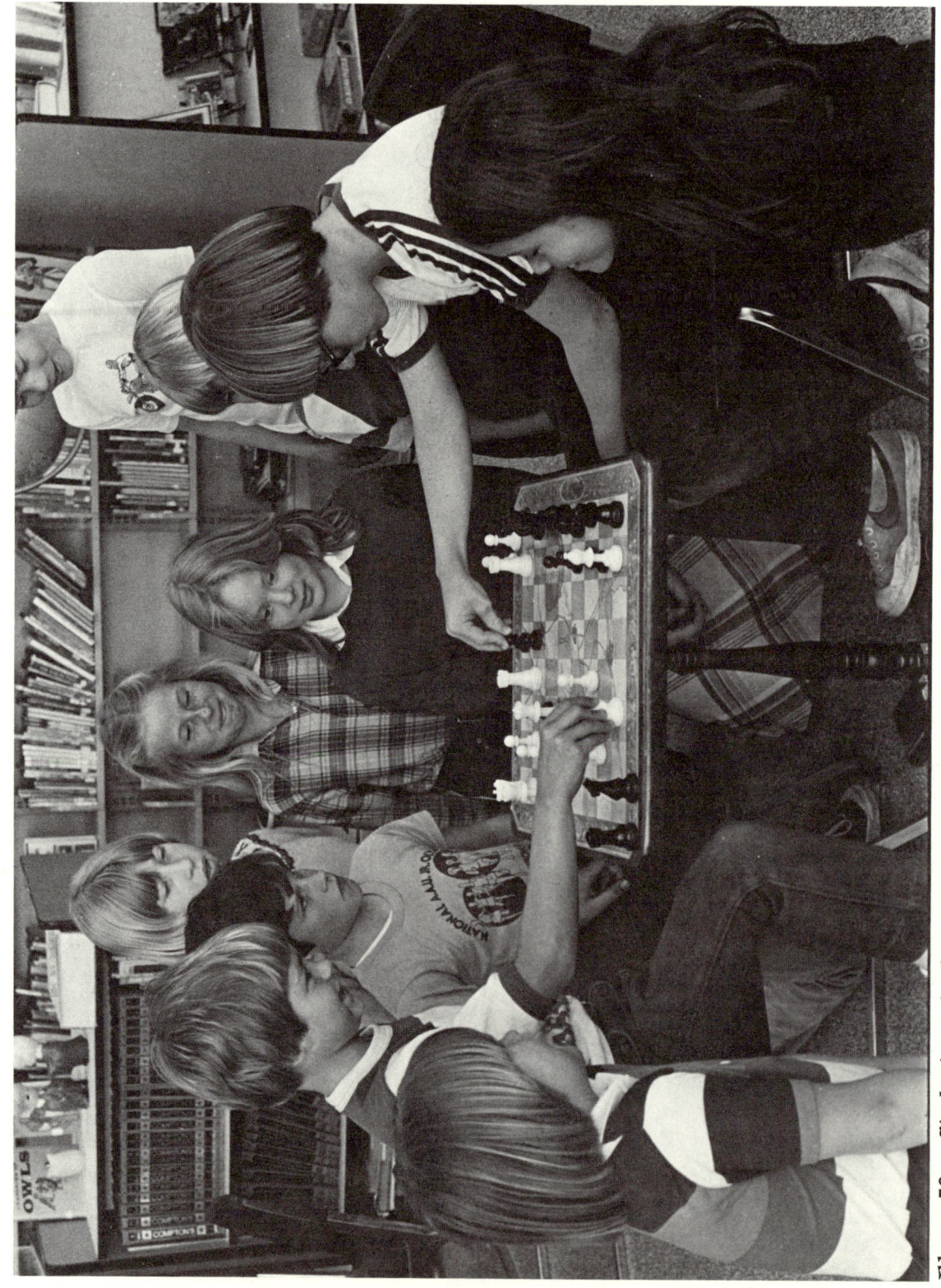

Illus. 59: Students enjoying recycled chess game

59. RECYCLING GAMES: CHESS

Participants: Media specialist; students

Location: Media center

Time span: 30-45 minutes

Purposes:
1) To provide a beneficial after-school activity
2) To stimulate interest in the media center
3) To stimulate thinking ability

Materials:
Chessboard (recycled)
Chess set (recycled)

Procedure:
1) Ask Parent Teacher Organization to solicit donations of used but complete chess sets to the media center.
2) Collect as many sets as possible.
3) Students play chess after school.

Suggestions:
1) This game is very popular with students, so several sets are needed.

60. RECYCLING GAMES: SCRABBLE

Participants: Media specialist; students

Location: Media center

Time span: During school day

Purposes:
1) To provide a beneficial library activity
2) To stimulate interest in the library center
3) To stimulate thinking ability

Materials: Scrabble game (recycled)

Procedure:
1) Ask Parent Teacher Organization to solicit donations of scrabble games to the media center.
2) Place game in the center of a library table.
3) Permit students to play any time during school day.

Suggestions: 1) Scrabble may be used as an after-school activity.

61. RECYCLING LOOSELEAF BINDERS: RECORD OF BIBLIOGRAPHIES

Participants:	Media specialist
Location:	Media center
Time span:	10 minutes
Purposes:	1) To preserve a copy of each bibliography for future reference
Materials:	Bibliographies Hole punch Looseleaf binder
Procedure:	1) Punch holes in bibliographies to correspond to rings in looseleaf binder. 2) Place bibliographies in looseleaf binder.
Suggestions:	1) Date each bibliography and the number of copies distributed.

62. RECYCLING LOOSELEAF BINDERS: RECORD OF INSTRUCTION DITTOS

Participants: Media specialist

Location: Media center

Time span: 10 minutes

Purposes: 1) To preserve a copy of each instructional ditto for future reference

Materials: Hole punch
Instructional dittos
Looseleaf binder

Procedure: 1) Punch holes in instructional dittos to correspond to rings in looseleaf binder.
2) Place dittos in looseleaf binder.

Suggestions: 1) Record on each ditto the grade level and number of classes instructed.

63. RECYCLING LOOSELEAF BINDERS: STORAGE FOR THEATER-IN-ROUND SCRIPTS

Participants: Media specialist

Location: Media center

Time span: 10 minutes

Purposes: 1) To store extra scripts for future use

Materials: Hole punch
Looseleaf binder
Scripts

Procedure: 1) Punch holes in scripts to correspond to rings in looseleaf binder.
2) Place scripts in looseleaf binder.

Suggestions: 1) Keep one copy of each play written in the media center; some students prefer to use a play already written and tried.

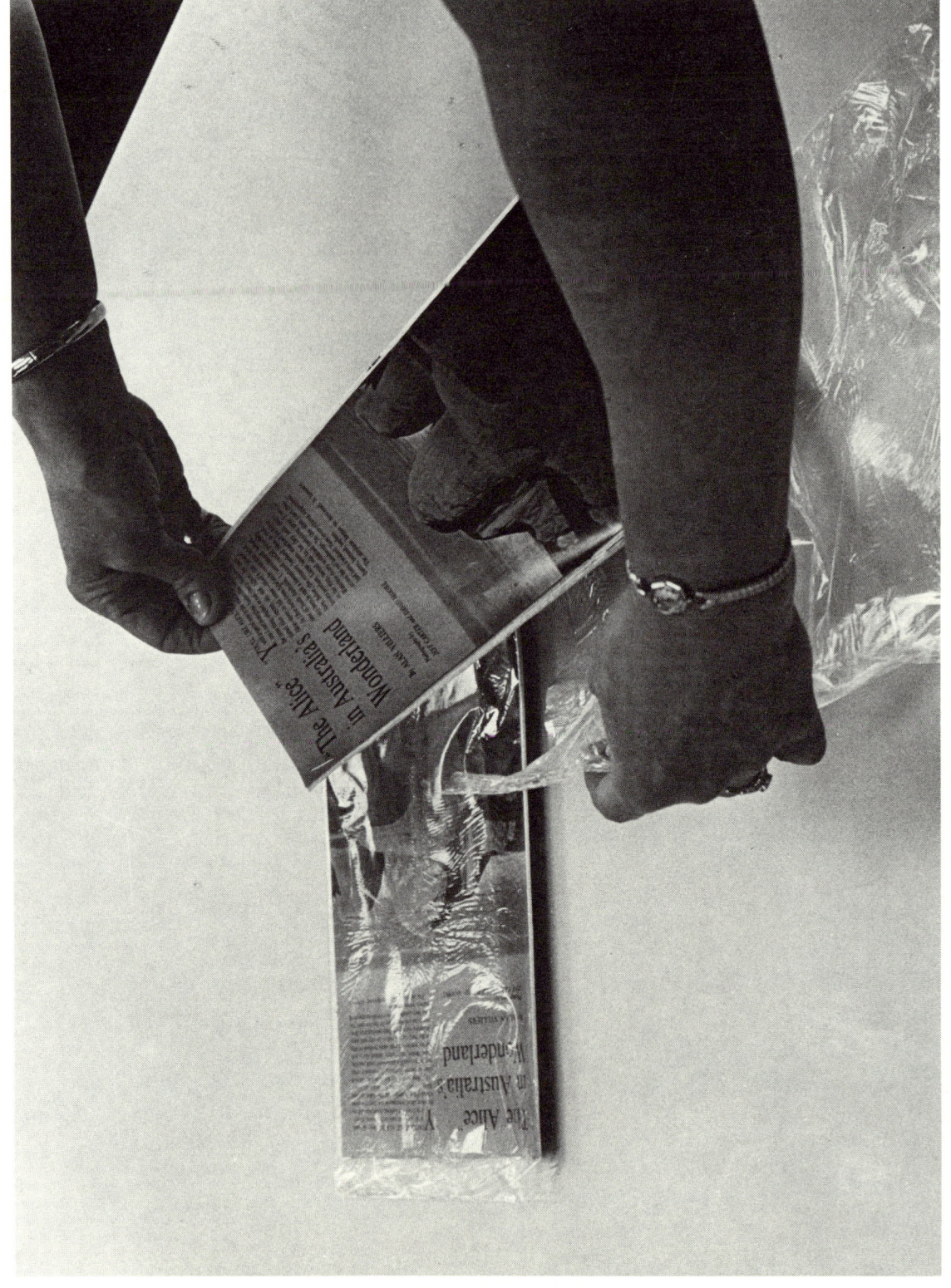

Illus. 64: Magazine articles make good vertical-file additions

64. RECYCLING MAGAZINES: MAGAZINE ARTICLES FOR VERTICAL FILE

Participants: Media specialists; parent assistants

Location: Media center

Time span: 30-45 minutes

Purposes:
1) To provide educational materials for student and faculty use
2) To provide additional sources of materials for student research projects

Materials:
Labels
Magazines (such as National Geographic, National Geographic World, etc.)
Staple remover
Stapler
Zip-lock baggies (or other plastic bags)

Procedure:
1) Remove staples from spine of magazine.
2) Separate articles.
3) Choose articles to be retained.
4) Staple each article separately.
5) Place each article in zip-lock baggie.
6) Label each baggie as to contents.
7) File each baggie in its appropriate spot in vertical file.

Suggestions:
1) Be selective in the choice of magazines to be used; the above procedure takes much time and effort.
2) Permit students and faculty to borrow and use these materials in classroom as well as home.

65. RECYCLING MAGAZINES: MAGAZINE GIVEAWAY

Participants: Media specialist; students

Location: Media center

Time span: 30 minutes

Purposes:
1) To discourage students from cutting out pictures from new magazines
2) To help students gather pictures for reports

Materials: Carton box
Magazines

Procedure:
1) Gather old magazines that cannot be stored in center (no room).
2) Remove book pockets and cards from magazines and destroy them.
3) Place magazines in carton box.
4) Write on sides of box: TAKE ME. I'M FREE.
5) Place box in a spot easily seen by students.

Suggestions:
1) Students love free materials. It may be necessary to restrict the number of free magazines each student may take.

66. RECYCLING MAPS: MAPS FOR STUDENT BORROWING

Participants: Media specialist; parent assistant

Location: Media center

Time span: 20-30 minutes

Purposes: 1) To provide maps that students may borrow

Materials: Book cards and pockets
Envelopes (appropriate size)
Maps (from discarded books, National Geographic magazines, newspapers, etc.)
Scotch tape

Procedure:
1) Gather all supplies to be used.
2) Gather maps to be retained.
3) Place each map in a separate envelope.
4) Type a pocket and a card for each map containing title of map and copy number.
5) Attach pocket and card to envelope with scotch tape.
6) Place envelopes containing maps in an attractive box.
7) Place box on atlas stand.

Suggestions:
1) Do not catalog maps, as they disappear quickly and therefore will not become part of your permanent collection.
2) Report-card envelopes make good packaging (see idea 78).

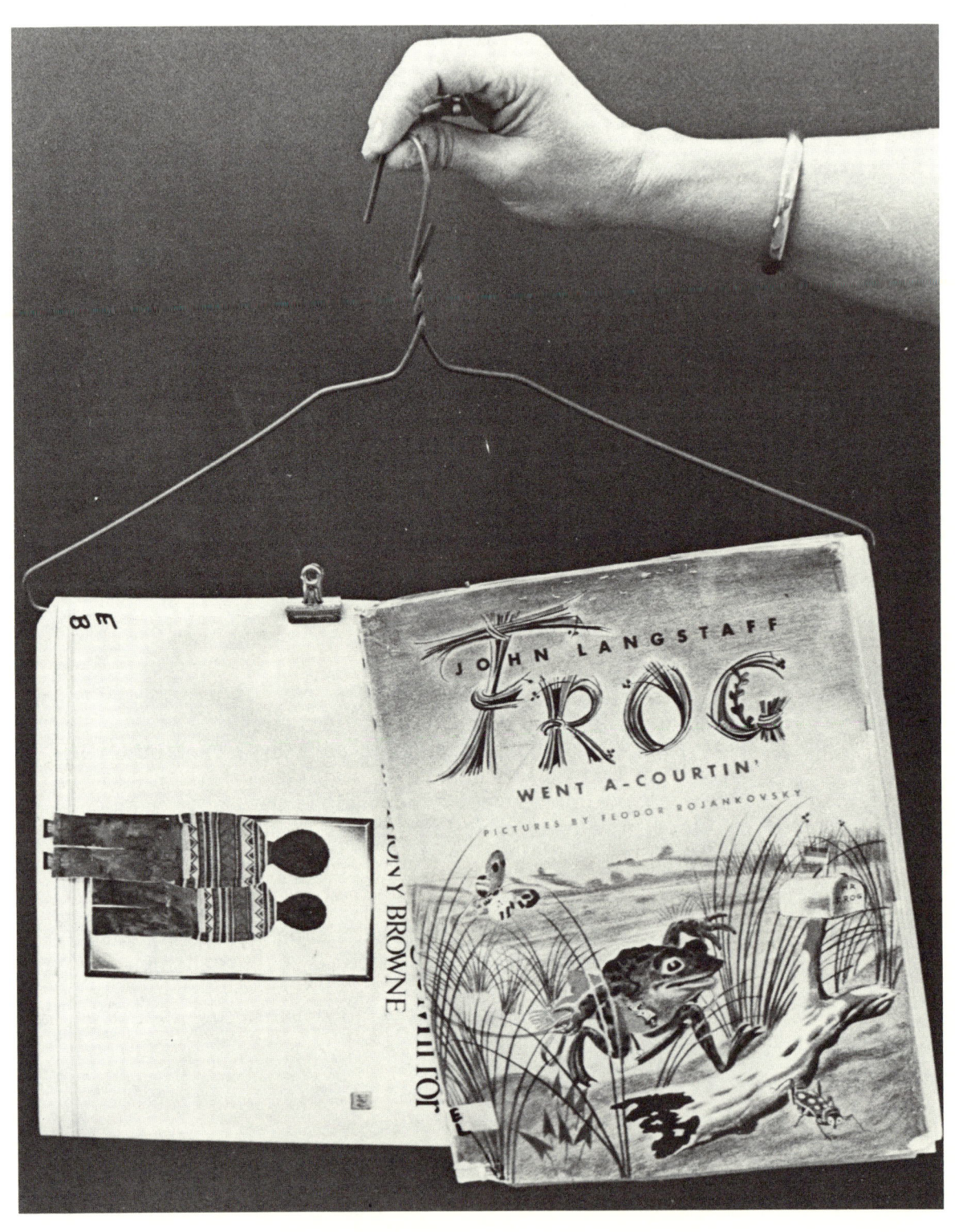

Illus. 67:
Book-jacket mobile ready to hand

67. RECYCLING NEWSPAPERS: BOOK-JACKET MOBILE

Participants: Media specialist; parent assistant

Location: Media center

Time span: 15 minutes

Purposes:
1) To entice students to read
2) To provide an attractive and meaningful decoration
3) To remind students of the many materials that can be recycled

Materials:
Book jackets
Cord
Newspapers
Stapler
Wire hanger

Procedure:
1) Fold newspapers to fit the exact size of each book jacket.
2) Staple newspapers to inside of each book jacket so only the book jacket can be seen from the outside.
3) Fold each book jacket so it looks like it is covering a book; staple where necessary.
4) Attach book jackets to a wire hanger.
5) Hang from bookcase or any other place desired.

Suggestions: 1) Choose colorful book jackets.

Illus. 68: Newspaper cartoons stimulate students to create their own

108

68. RECYCLING NEWSPAPERS: MAKE YOUR OWN CARTOON

Participants: Media specialist; students

Location: Media center

Time span: 15 minutes

Purposes: 1) To provide fun activity for students

Materials: Cartoon section (Sunday or daily newspapers)
Ditto sheets (used)
Easel
Magic markers
Stapler
Tape

Procedure: 1) Tape cartoon sections to front of easel.
2) Staple used ditto sheets together as a pad.
3) Set out a set of magic markers.
4) Add a sign: CREATE A CARTOON.

Suggestions: 1) Cartoons created by students make an interesting bulletin board.

69. RECYCLING NEWSPAPERS: NEWSPAPER CLIPPINGS

Participants: Media specialist; parent assistant; students

Location: Media center

Time span: 30 minutes

Purposes:
1) To educate students to the value of newspapers as resources
2) To enlarge the collection of instructional materials available to students and teachers
3) To encourage students to read newspapers

Materials:
Envelopes (manila, small)
Newspapers
Scissors

Procedure:
1) Gather newspapers of previous week.
2) Glean through newspapers for articles that can be used for instruction or research.
3) Cut out appropriate articles.
4) Place each clipping in an envelope; indicate contents of envelope by pen.
5) File envelopes in vertical file.

Suggestions:
1) Involve 4th- and 5th-grade students in this activity by arrangement with classroom teachers.

70. RECYCLING NEWSPAPERS: TABLETOP PROTECTION

Participants: Media specialist

Location: Media center

Time span: 5 minutes

Purposes: 1) To protect tabletops during production of puppets and other messy projects and activities

Materials: Newspaper

Procedure: 1) Cover tabletop with newspaper before activity begins.
2) Throw newspaper away after activity is completed if it is messy.

Suggestions: 1) Keep newspaper if it can be used again.

71. RECYCLING NEWSPAPERS: THAT WAS THE WEEK THAT WAS

Participants:	Media specialist; parent assistant
Location:	Media center
Time span:	15 minutes
Purposes:	1) To encourage students to read newspapers 2) To make students aware of the importance of knowing current events
Materials:	Newspapers (daily; Sunday) Tape
Procedure:	1) Gather previous week's newspapers. 2) Cover carrel walls with newspaper taped in place. 3) Arrange newspapers neatly in one or two piles in carrel. 4) Attach sign: THAT WAS THE WEEK THAT WAS.
Suggestions:	1) Effective in grades 4, 5.

Illus. 72: Reading corner created with pillow

72. RECYCLING PILLOWS: READING CORNER

Participants:	Media specialist
Location:	Media center
Time span:	10 minutes
Purposes:	1) To encourage reading 2) To provide quiet spot in which to read
Materials:	Pillow (large, recycled) Pillow case (large, recycled)
Procedure:	1) Ask Parent Teacher Organization to solicit donations of large pillows and pillowcases members wish to get rid of. 2) Select quiet, protected, inviting nook. 3) Place pillow, covered with attractive pillowcase, on the floor of the nook.
Suggestions:	1) Students love reading corners. Start with one and add others as needed.

Illus. 73: Plastic cups and lids as Christmas-tree decorations

73. RECYCLING PLASTIC CUPS: CHRISTMAS-TREE BELLS

Participants: Media specialist; students

Location: Media center

Time span: 10 minutes

Purposes: 1) To provide fun holiday activity for students

Materials: Cord
Paper clips
Pictures (small, magazine)
Plastic cups (coffee)
Scissors
Scotch tape

Procedure: 1) Gather cups; wash and dry them.
2) Cut out appropriate pictures from old magazines.
3) Each student receives cup and picture.
4) Each student tapes picture to inside or outside of cup.
5) Each student pokes two small holes with scissors through bottom of cup.
6) Each student inserts a paper clip or cord through holes.
7) Each student hangs cup on Christmas tree.

Suggestions: 1) Good as an individual or small-group activity.

74. RECYCLING PLASTIC HOSE EGGS: EASTER EGGS

Participants: Media specialist; students

Location: Media center

Time span: 10 minutes

Purposes: 1) To provide fun activity for students

Materials: Egg-shaped containers (hosiery)
Magic markers
Paper (colored)
Scissors
Scotch tape

Procedure: 1) Place materials in a box in the center of a table.
2) Any student may make an Easter egg.
3) Individual students select hose containers.
4) They draw appropriate pictures on colored paper.
5) Pictures are cut out and attached to containers with scotch tape.
6) Students may keep their Easter eggs.

Suggestions: 1) Students enjoy making these simple Easter eggs, so many egg-shaped hose containers are needed.

75. RECYCLING PLASTIC LIDS: CHRISTMAS-TREE ORNAMENTS

Participants: Media specialist; students

Location: Media center

Time span: 10 minutes

Purposes: 1) To provide fun activity for students

Materials: Magic markers
Paper clips
Plastic lids

Procedure:
1) Set materials in box on table close to Christmas tree.
2) Any student may make ornament and attach it to tree.
3) Student draws appropriate design with magic marker on one side of lid; allow to dry.
4) Student turns lid over and draws design; allow to dry.
5) Student pokes hole through lid close to top.
6) Student inserts paper clip through hole, creating hook.
7) Student hangs decorated lid on Christmas tree.

Suggestions:
1) Decorated lids can also be used as window ornaments.
2) See illus. 73 for other Christmas-tree ornaments.

76. RECYCLING PUZZLES: PUZZLES FOR HOME USE

Participants: Media specialist; students

Location: Media center

Time span: 10 minutes

Purposes:
1) To provide thinking activity for students
2) To provide take-home learning activity for students

Materials:
Book card
Book pocket
Date-due slip
Puzzle (recycled)

Procedure:
1) Ask Parent Teacher Organization to solicit donations of unwanted but complete puzzles to the media center.
2) Do not catalog puzzles.
3) Attach date-due slip, card pocket, and book card to puzzle box.
4) Place puzzle in noticeable spot.
5) Repeat above procedure for each puzzle.
6) Permit students to borrow puzzles, using the same borrowing procedure as books.

Suggestions: 1) See illus. 1.

77. RECYCLING RECORDS: BACKGROUND MUSIC

Participants:	Media specialist; students
Location:	Media center
Time span:	Daily
Purposes:	1) To provide pleasant atmosphere 2) To acquaint students with classical music 3) To introduce students to theater music
Materials:	Phonograph Records (donated) Tote box
Procedure:	1) Place records in tote box. 2) Place phonograph and tote box in carrel. 3) Permit students to choose records to play.
Suggestions:	1) Solicit donations through Parent Teacher Organizations. 2) Screen records carefully and retain only what you wish to use.

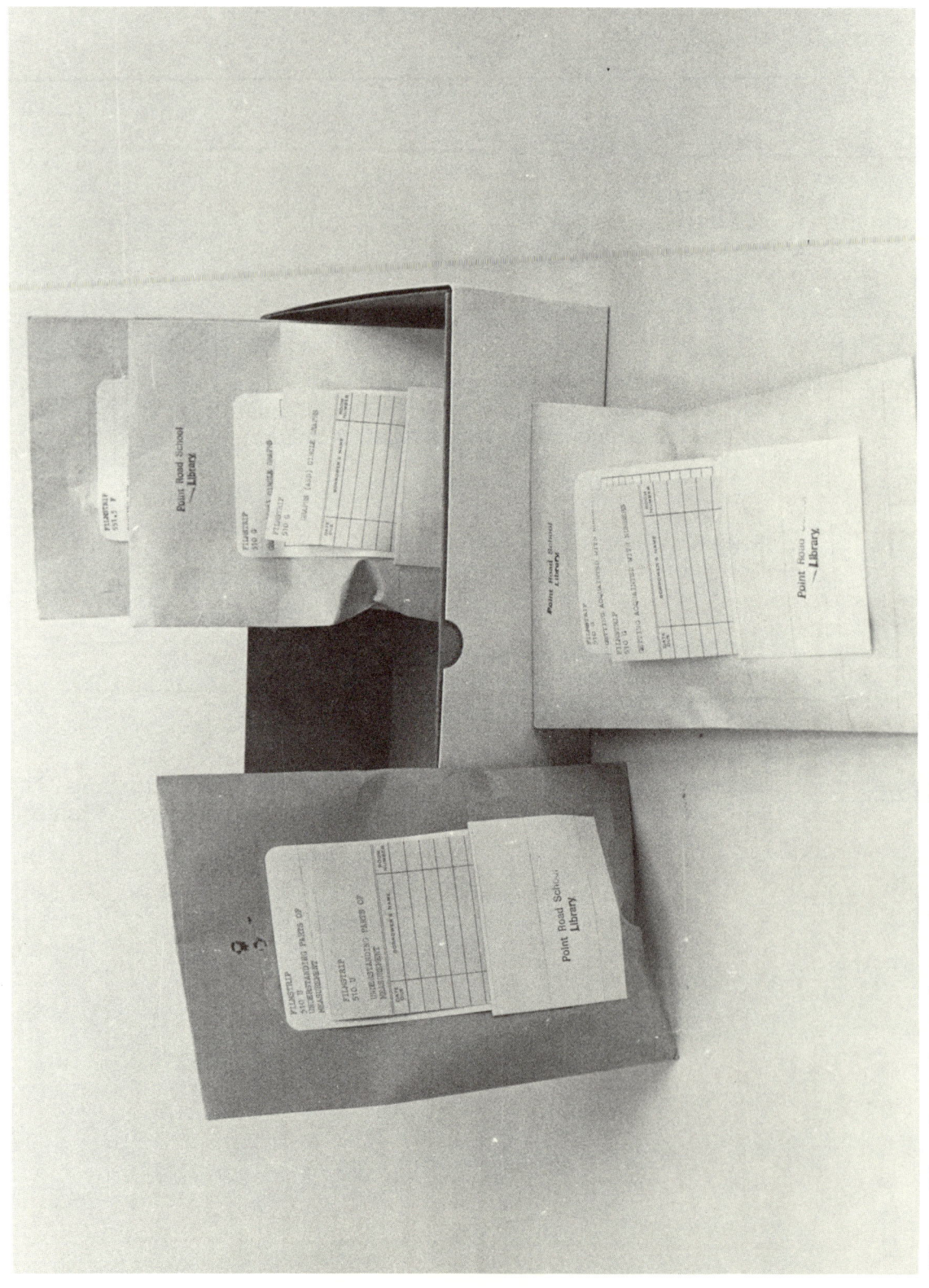

Illus. 78: Report-card envelopes as AV packaging

78. RECYCLING REPORT-CARD ENVELOPES: AV CONTAINERS

Participants:	Media specialist; parent assistant
Location:	Media center
Time span:	10 minutes
Purposes:	1) To facilitate borrowing of AV materials 2) To provide easy storage for AV materials 3) To facilitate organization of AV materials
Materials:	Book card Book pocket Report-card envelope (discontinued)
Procedure:	1) Type number, title, and copy number of AV material on both book pocket and book card. 2) Tape pocket to envelope; insert card. 3) Slip AV material into envelope and place on proper shelf.
Suggestions:	1) Recycled report-card envelopes can hold filmstrips, maps, c cassette tapes, etc. 2) Check with your Board of Education office. There may be boxes of envelopes for discontinued report cards that you can obtain for free.

Illus. 79: Album of owl pictures, stories, and poems

79. RECYCLING SCRAPBOOK COVERS: SPECIAL ALBUM

Participants: Media specialist; students

Location: Media center

Time span: 15 minutes

Purposes: 1) To provide book in which to mount original student pictures, poems, and stories

Materials: Covers (scrapbook or photograph album)
Magic marker
Paper (construction)
Scotch tape

Procedure:
1) Wipe album covers with damp cloth to remove dust and dirt.
2) Insert construction paper.
3) Print with magic marker on cover: PICTURES, STORIES, POEMS.
4) Mount poems, pictures, stories with scotch tape.

Suggestions:
1) A media-center symbol makes good theme for student pictures, stories, poems.
2) Exhibit book for the whole school to appreciate.

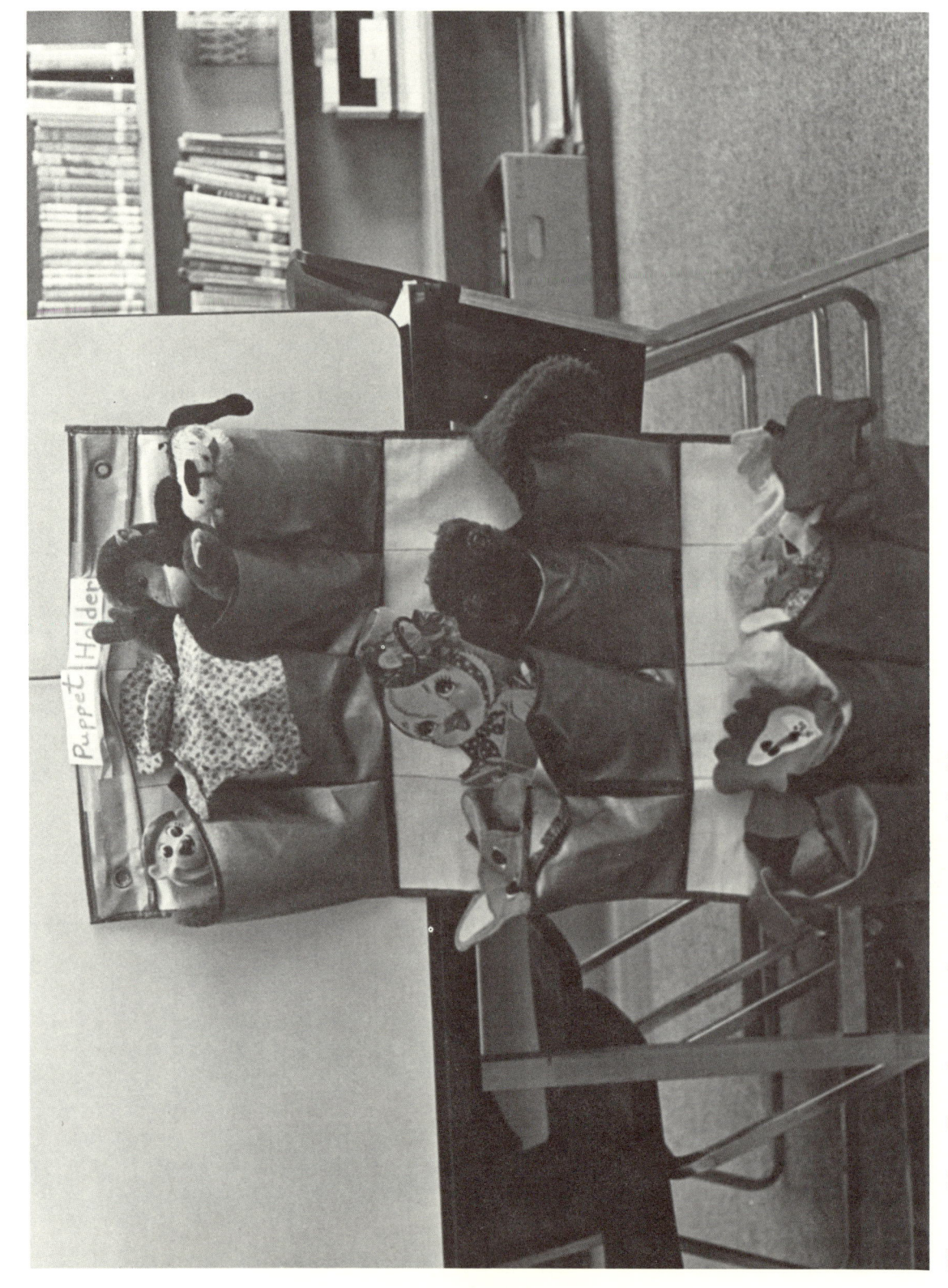

Illus. 80: Shoe bag used as a puppet holder

80. RECYCLING SHOE BAGS: PUPPET HOLDER

Participants: Media specialist

Location: Media center

Time span: 10 minutes

Purposes: 1) To provide attractive storage area for puppets
2) To provide easy access to puppets

Materials: Magic marker (black)
Puppets
Shoe bag
Wire hanger

Procedure: 1) Print on shoe bag with magic marker: PUPPET HOLDER.
2) Hang shoe bag on wire hanger.
3) Hang wire hanger inside puppet stage or wherever convenient.
4) Fill each pocket with puppet.

Suggestions: 1) Recycled shoe bag can also hold dolls or stuffed animals.

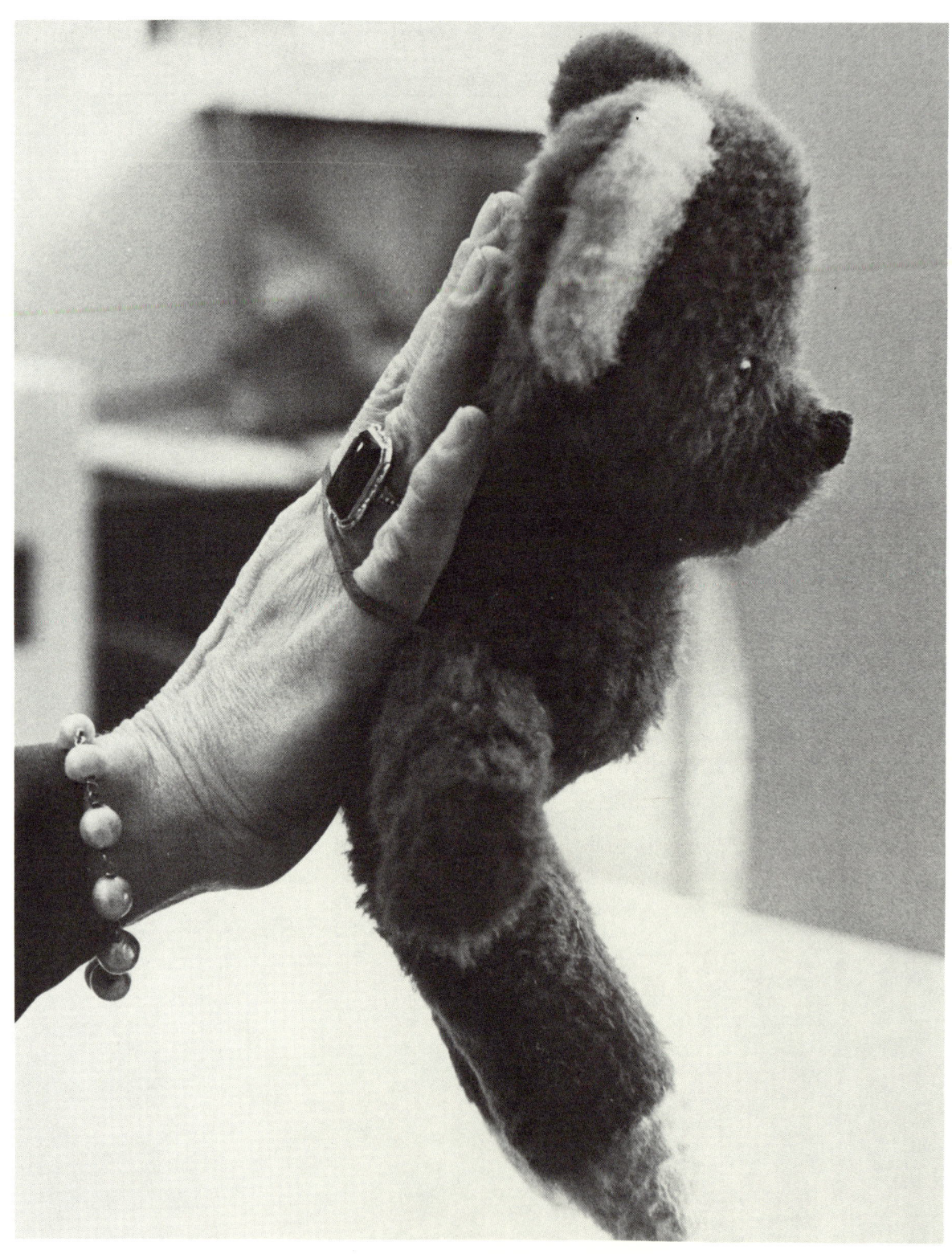

Illus. 81: Stuffed animal helps tell a story

81. RECYCLING STUFFED ANIMALS: STORYTELLING WITH STUFFED ANIMALS

Participants:	Media specialist
Location:	Media center
Time span:	15 minutes
Purposes:	1) To stimulate interest in stories 2) To stimulate the imagination of students
Materials:	Rubber band Stuffed animal (recycled)
Procedure:	1) Ask Parent Teacher Organization to solicit donations of unwanted stuffed animals to media center. 2) Choose animal to use in storytelling. 3) Seat students on rug. 4) Introduce story. 5) Attach stuffed animal to hand with rubber band. 6) Sit on a low storytelling stool. 7) Tell story. 8) Have stuffed animal help tell story.
Suggestions:	1) Requires practice to carry on a dialogue between storyteller and stuffed animal. 2) Effective in K-3.

82. RECYCLING SUITCASES: COSTUME COLLECTION

Participants: Media specialist; students

Location: Media center

Time span: 15 minutes

Purposes:
1) To store costumes in smallest amount of space
2) To move costume collection easily whenever it is needed

Materials:
Costumes (donated)
Magic marker (black)
Suitcase (donated)

Procedure:
1) Gather suitcase and costumes.
2) Print with magic marker on sides of suitcase: COSTUME COLLECTION.
3) Open suitcase and place costumes neatly inside.
4) Permit students to look through and use costumes for school plays.

Suggestions:
1) A large carton may be substituted for suitcase.
2) For costumes see illus. 39, 41A, 41B.

83. RECYCLING SUITCASES: ENVIRONMENTAL KIT

Participants: Media specialist

Location: Media center

Time span: 15 minutes

Purposes:
1) To gather environmental materials in one area
2) To use least amount of space
3) To be able to carry materials to other buildings
4) To be able to carry materials to classrooms

Materials: Environmental materials (booklets, pictures, etc.)
Magic marker (black)
Suitcase (old)

Procedure:
1) Gather environmental materials and suitcase.
2) Print with magic marker on each side of suitcase: ENVIRONMENTAL KIT.
3) Arrange materials neatly inside suitcase.
4) Acquaint teachers with Environmental Kit.

Suggestions: 1) Ask students to carry this kit to classrooms when needed.

84. RECYCLING SUITCASES: PUPPET STORAGE

Participants: Media specialist; students

Location: Media center

Time span: 10 minutes

Purposes:
1) To gather puppets into one area
2) To be able to carry puppet collection to classrooms easily

Materials:
Magic marker (black)
Puppets
Suitcase (old)

Procedure:
1) Print with magic marker on both sides of suitcase: PUPPET COLLECTION.
2) Arrange puppets neatly inside suitcase.
3) Place suitcase in appropriate area for student use.

Suggestions:
1) A large box may be substituted for suitcase.

85. RECYCLING WIRE HANGERS: DISPLAY

Participants: Media specialist; classroom teacher

Location: Media center; classroom

Time span: As needed

Purposes: 1) To display student creations

Materials: Cord
Finished projects
Wire hangers

Procedure: 1) Hang finished projects on wire hangers with cord.
2) Hang wire hangers in appropriate area.

Suggestions: 1) Wire hangers have many uses, including displaying mobiles, hanging costumes to keep them neat, displaying Christmas decorations, and holding brown bags for book protectors.
2) See illus. 16, 28, 67, 80.

Illus. 86: Puzzle board created from unwanted piece of wood

86. RECYCLING WOOD BOARDS: PUZZLE BOARD

Participants:	Media specialist
Location:	Media center
Time span:	10 minutes
Purposes:	1) To provide a place where students can leave unfinished puzzles to which they can return
Materials:	Board (wood) Magic marker Paper (colored) Sandpaper Tape
Procedure:	1) Choose board of appropriate size and shape. 2) Use sandpaper to remove splinters and dirt spots. 3) Cover board with colored paper; tape colored paper to board. 4) Print on board: PUZZLE BOARD. 5) Place on table for student use.
Suggestions:	1) A cardboard or game board may be substituted.

INDEX

[Numbers refer to project, not page.]

ALBUMS
    Special album 79

ART
    For home use 1

AV STORAGE
    Boxes 14
    Report-card envelopes 78
    Study-print envelopes 24

BOOK REPORTS
    Dioramas 12
    With costumes 38

BOOKS
    Feltboard stories 2
    Paperback and cassette set 6
    Paperback exchange 3
    Storyteller's file 4
    Tracing pictures 5

BOTTLES
    Candlestick 7
    Finger puppets 8
    Flower vases 9
    Terrarium 10

BOXES
    Book holders 11
    Dioramas 12
    Finger-puppet stage 13
    Storage 14
    Theater-in-Round props 15

BROWN BAGS
    Book protectors 16
    Masks 17

CALENDARS
    Tracing calendar pictures 18

CANDLES
    Story-hour candle 19

CANDLESTICKS
    From bottle 7

CARD CATALOG
    Scrap sheets 45

CARDBOARD
    Animal costuming 20
    Christmas-tree birds 21
    Body puppets 22
    Feltboard making 23
    Puppet making--outline form 25
    Puppet-storage hand 26
    Puzzle making 27
    Story mobiles 28
    Study-print envelopes 24

CARDBOARD TUBES
    Puppet making--construction
      paper 29
    Repair caddy 30

CASSETTE TAPES
    For home use of particular

    students 32
    Interest centers 33
    Music-listening station 34
    Paperback and cassette set 6
    Theater-in-Round sound effects 35

CATALOGS
    Picture tracing 36

CHRISTMAS TREE
    Bells 73
    Birds 21
    Ornaments 75

CLOTH
    Puppets 37

COSTUMES
    Book reports 38
    Collection 39
    Storyteller's costume 40
    Theater-in-Round 41

CROCKERY
    Planters 42

CURTAINS
    Puppet stage 43

DECORATIONS
    Christmas-tree bells 73
    Christmas-tree birds 21
    Easter eggs 74
    Flower vases 9
    Terrariums 10

DITTO SHEETS
    Card-catalog scrap sheets 45
    Ditto doodle pad 46
    Doodle display 47
    Make your own bookmarks 48
    Puppet-play writing--rough copy 49
    Theater-in-Round play writing--rough copy 50

DOLLS
    Storytelling with 51

DOODLE
    Display 47
    Pad 46

EASTER
    Eggs 74

EGG CARTONS
    Finger-puppet storage 52
    Organizer tray 53
    Walking storybook characters 54

FELTBOARD
    Making 23
    Stories 2

FOAM PLASTIC
    Book holder 55
    Organizer tray 56

GAMES
    Backgammon 57
    Checkers 58
    Chess 59
    Scrabble 60

LOOSELEAF BINDERS
    Record of bibliographies 61
    Record of instruction dittos 62
    Storage for Theater-in-Round scripts 63

MAGAZINES
    Articles for vertical file 64
    Giveaway 65

MAPS
    For student borrowing 66

MOBILES
    Book jacket 67
    Story 28

MUSIC
    Background 77
    Listening station 34

NEWSPAPERS
    Book-jacket mobile 67
    Make your own cartoon 68
    Newspaper clippings 69
    Tabletop protection 70
    That was the week that was 71

PAPERBACKS
    Exchange 3
    Paperback and cassette set 6

PILLOWS
    Reading corner 72

PLASTIC CUPS
    Christmas-tree bells 73

PLASTIC EGG CONTAINERS
    Easter eggs 74

PLASTIC LIDS
    Christmas-tree ornaments 75

PUPPETRY
    Body puppets 22
    Finger puppets 37
    Finger-puppet stage 13
    Puppet making--construction paper 29
    Puppet making--outline form 25
    Puppet-play writing--rough copy 49
    Puppet-stage curtain 43
    Puppet storage 84
    Puppet-storage hand 26
    Puppets (cloth) 37

PUZZLES
    For home use 76
    Puzzle board 86
    Puzzle making 27

REPORT-CARD ENVELOPES
    AV containers 78

SCRAPBOOKS
    Special album 79

SHOE BAGS
    Puppet holder 80

STORYTELLING
    Candle 19
    Candlestick 7
    Feltboard making 23
    Feltboard stories 2
    Storyteller's costume 40
    Storyteller's file 4
    Storytelling with doll 51
    Storytelling with stuffed animals 81

STUFFED ANIMALS
    Storytelling with 81

SUITCASE
    Costume collection 82
    Environmental kit 83
    Puppet storage 84

THEATER-IN-ROUND
    Animal costuming 20
    Costume collection 39
    Script writing--rough copy 50
    Sound effects 35

VERTICAL FILE
    Magazine articles 64
    Newspaper clippings 69

WIRE HANGERS
    Book-jacket mobile 67
    Display 85
    Story mobile 28

WOOD
    Puzzle board 86